WILDLIFE *of the* PENNINE HILLS

First published in Great Britain by Merlin Unwin Books Ltd 2019

Merlin Unwin Books Ltd
Palmers House
7 Corve Street
Ludlow
Shropshire SY8 1DB
UK

www.merlinunwin.co.uk

ISBN 978-1-910723-96-8

Typeset in 11 point Bembo by Merlin Unwin
Printed by DZS Grafik

WILDLIFE *of the* PENNINE HILLS

MOORLAND • LIMESTONE • GRASSLAND • WOODLAND • BLANKET BOG • UPLAND HEATH

Doug Kennedy

Merlin Unwin Books

Black grouse in flight

CONTENTS

Heather moorland at Langsett, West Yorkshire with millstone grit boulders

INTRODUCTION

This book is about nature in the Pennine Hills of England. It explores the countryside through the wildlife that is to be found there, and how the wildlife relates to the geology and conditions found in the various Pennine landscapes. We hope that this focus on natural history will add an extra dimension to the pleasure of exploring the hills. The beautiful photographic images provide a visual guide to what to look out for in each of the different habitats and assist with identifying plants and animals that can be encountered there. *Wildlife in the Pennine Hills* is not intended to be a field guide but considers the natural history of these hills more holistically, exploring how the geology and landscapes support the life forms that live there and how they all interact. I hope it will deepen the reader's understanding and appreciation of what lives within the Pennines and why it is there.

Running in a continuous range up the middle of the country, the Pennine Hills are often referred to as the 'backbone of England', more or less dividing the northern half of England into east and west, from the Potteries in Staffordshire to the Tyne Gap in Northumberland (please see page 14 for the area covered by this book). Of course, the precise extent and boundaries of a geographical feature such as the Pennines is subject to interpretation and even local custom or practice: for instance, the Pennine Way long-distance walking route extends far north of the Tyne Gap to Kirk Yetholm on the Scottish side of the border.

The Pennine landscape is characterised by moorland rising to its highest point at Cross Fell in eastern Cumbria, at 2,930 feet (893m), but there is a variety of other landscapes whose presence usually depends upon the underlying geology and the altitude.

The habitats explored in this book are divided into blanket bogs, upland heaths, limestone landscapes, grasslands, woodlands and waterbodies, each of which provides a specific set of conditions, inhabited predominantly by plants and animals that are specialists, suited to living there. In addition, the Pennines are intersected by river valleys, the largest of which contain farmland, settlements and transport corridors: in such places, the conditions have been changed by human activity, so the wildlife that remains may be less typical of any habitat type, making them less suitable for description in this book.

The range of specialist flora and fauna found in each habitat type is the focus of this book. I seek to explain why each plant or animal is suited to living in its particular habitat, and most are illustrated by photographs. Common species which are to be found all across England are not explored in detail. These generalist species are likely to be particularly in evidence as you pass through the lowland woods and grasslands, especially when there are farms and settlements close by.

One habitat is not always easily distinguished from the next, for instance when upland heath merges into wet heath then blanket bog, all of which may have been modified in the interests of outdoor pursuits such as grouse shooting. Nature is chaotic and doesn't like purity or straight lines, so working out which actual habitat type you are passing through can be less than straightforward. In addition, organisms don't necessarily stick to where they are theoretically supposed to occur, and some appear in unexpected places because of a temporary food source or weather conditions. As a result, this book should be treated as a rough guide to the location of any organism along with accurate species-specific information. This book will, hopefully, give the reader a feel for the range and type of wildlife within each habitat and an insight into the natural order that exists in each case.

I am exploring the Pennine range by habitat type, rather than geography, so the description of wildlife in the blanket bogs or the upland heaths could apply anywhere over the distance from Edale to Hexhamshire Common. This is because the general habitat conditions are likely to be similar as will be the range of organisms that live there. Limestone habitats are somewhat more individual, with

Ruined farmhouse of Top Withens on Howarth Moor

different conditions applying in each area, so that chapter is subdivided into the Peak District, the Yorkshire Dales and Upper Teesdale.

The first habitat type covered is blanket bog which, in the case of the Pennines, covers the highest and most inaccessible land. Blanket bog is in the high places because it sits on a plateau of impermeable millstone grit on which water collects and conditions are challenging for both plants and animals so the number of species is quite limited and well-defined. True blanket bog is very difficult to cross or to build on and will therefore often be in its natural state, uninterfered with in recent times.

The second habitat type is upland heath. This normally occurs just below blanket bog and can extend down the lower slopes. These two habitats may both occur together in a single area and one can become the other if conditions change. Heath dominates much of the Pennine moorland where the soil is too poor for agriculture but not as wet or acidic as in the blanket bogs. Whether the land is green pasture, white moor or reed-strewn bog usually depends on land management, for instance through drainage, sheep pasturing or fertilising.

Limestone habitats follow, which represent a strong contrast to the moors and bogs surrounding them, mostly because of the interaction of water with the bedrock. Limestone turns water slightly alkaline, which results in different plant species. The limestone is dissolved by water which has created some very distinctive landscapes and means that there is little surface water, as cracks in the rock allow it to descend into the bedrock where many waterways flow through underground caverns, often emerging many miles away. The limestone bedrock is not as high as the millstone grit so most of the land is farmed, whilst unimproved limestone areas are, generally, where the land is too rocky or steep to be farmed. Intensive livestock farming is most common and this reduces the diversity of native species, which has meant that some habitats, particularly wildflower meadows, have become very scarce. However where the limestone land has been unintensively managed, it can be very rich in plant species.

Grasslands are the focus of Chapter 4, and in the Pennines these extend from ryegrass monocultures in the intensively farmed lowlands to long stretches of semi-natural upland grazing and also to the rare, unimproved flower meadows. The focus of the Pennine Grasslands chapter is, once again, on native wildlife which is typical of its habitat, so although actively farmed grassland is extremely common across the lower slopes of the range, it is the rare flower meadows and the higher places where there is less human intervention that are discussed in detail.

When most people think of the Pennines, it is the open moors that come to mind rather than forests, so names such as the 'Forest of Trawden' can be deceptive, as the area is mostly devoid of trees and its name derives from its days as a hunting park. There are, however, many woods spread throughout the area, the great majority of which are quite small in extent and found on the slopes rather than on the tops of the range. This is because of the harsh conditions on higher ground: cold temperatures, high winds and poor, wet soils, especially in exposed locations.

Trees thrive in more protected locations, even the rocky valleys (or dales) where the wind is less destructive and soil can build up to support tree growth. The Woodlands chapter is split into sandstone and limestone habitats because the bedrock affects the acidity of soil and water which, in turn, determines which tree species can thrive.

Native woodlands and older plantations are almost always comprised of mixed broadleafed species, contrasting sharply with coniferous plantations that were planted in the 20th century. These were often planted almost anywhere in order to secure government grants, with little regard for the underlying soil and geology, and as a result they are of variable quality. Most offer opportunities for native wildlife, so they are included.

The final habitat type described is aquatic: the rivers and waterbodies. The Pennine hills are a watershed for the Atlantic fronts that roll in and keep England green all year round, so a lot of rain falls on them. Some of this is absorbed by the bogs and moors, but most water must find a way down, creating the huge numbers of becks (streams) and rivers which are a major characteristic of these hills. There are, however, only two Pennine lakes and few tarns (ponds) of any size across their entire length because of the form of the land and the underlying geology. The many waterbodies which do exist are artificial reservoirs that were created in order to supply the huge spread of towns

Woodland and pasture in Manifold Dale

and industries that lie on the lower land to the east and west. The need to maintain a high purity in reservoir water has meant that development of the land above them is very carefully controlled, which has left the wide expanses of moorland open and largely unspoiled.

Many species of birds, fish and invertebrates are supported by the range of aquatic habitats, provided that the water quality is good. Sadly, pollution of waterways is a continuing problem which is explored in this chapter.

The Extent of the Pennine Hills

In the south, the Pennines rise up from north of the A50 road between Stoke-on-Trent and Derby. The rolling farmland rises from the Staffordshire Potteries to 370 metres altitude around Cauldon, and this is where the bedrock changes to the limestone of the so-called 'White Peak': this is also the southern boundary of The Peak District National Park. Here, the Rivers Hamps, Manifold

Howden Reservoir on the River Derwent, Derbyshire

Limestone pavement on Twistleton Scars in the Yorkshire Dales

and Dove have carved spectacular valleys into the bedrock whose steep slopes rise to where grey drystone walls criss-cross the green landscape. The White Peak extends north as far as Castleton and the Winnats Pass. It is a landscape characterised by livestock grazing on green farmland that is punctuated by grey limestone crags and by deep water-cut valleys. However, this is not the end of the story as, still within the National Park, the limestone is sandwiched between extensive areas to the east and west where the bedrock is millstone grit and the surface is covered by moorland.

To the north and east of Castleton, the bedrock is millstone grit and other hard sandstones which form the Dark Peak. Here the uplands are moorland fells which rise and fall in rounded hills crossed by dark sandstone walls with few trees. The soils are acidic, in contrast with the alkaline limestone in the White Peaks, so the colours are muted except when the heather is in bloom. In the high places, the moorland stretches for sixty miles north, broken only by river valleys which drain the Pennine chain to the east into Yorkshire, and west into Lancashire, and where the moss is replaced by settlements and farms. The northern extremity of the Peak District National Park is the Colne Valley which contains the River Colne along with its adjacent canal, and the A62 road linking Huddersfield and Manchester.

From there the millstone grit moorland continues north to Calderdale and Pendle Hill, to the north-west of which lies the Forest of Bowland: this is a westward extension of the Pennine gritstone with a similar landscape extending to within a few miles of the Lancashire coast.

The town of Skipton and the A59 road mark the start of the Yorkshire Dales whose national park extends 65 miles northward to the Greta Valley and the A66 road that runs between Brough and Scotch Corner. Most of the area within the Yorkshire Dales is spectacular limestone country where the stark scars of the karst rock formations rise to the heights of the three peaks of Great Whernside,

Ingleborough and Pen-y-Ghent. Here, it becomes clear that the limestone is capped by sandstone as dark rock is found atop the highest hills and along with the moors to the east.

To the west of the Dales, the steep, rounded Howgill Fells form another extension of the Pennines that links to the Lake District, nowadays across the M6 motorway. Their bedrock is a very ancient sandstone from the Coniston group, and they have quite a distinctive character so they are not discussed in this book, although the upland heath habitats will have similarities.

North of the A66, the North Pennines form a 40-odd mile square of deep limestone valleys capped by broad plateaux of gritstone moorland. One of these valleys is Upper Teesdale which contains some of the rarest and most unusual communities of plants in England.

The northern extremity of the Pennines is where they descend to the Tyne Gap and the A69 links Newcastle with Carlisle. To the north of this are the Cheviot Hills which continue through Northumberland and across Hadrian's Wall and the border into Scotland.

SOME BASIC GEOLOGY OF THE PENNINE HILLS

The story of the formation of the Pennines starts during the Carboniferous Period, which lasted from about 360 million years ago, and continues to the start of the Permian period at 298 million years ago. Before this, the land that now forms the Pennines was a shallow basin covered by an equatorial sea in which corals, diatoms and other shelled creatures thrived. As they died, their shells were deposited on the sea floor, building up huge deposits of calcium carbonate. Over millions of years, the Earth's crust moved and the climate changed. By around 320 million years ago, large rivers carried flows of grit and mud from the surrounding land into the sea, and this sank to the bottom, covering the remaining reefs and creating a new thick layer comprised mostly of silica rather than lime.

Time and the weight of covering material transformed the calcium deposits into limestone, and the upper layer into sandstone and, in particular, the hard Millstone Grit which now lies at the top of the Pennines. Over the hundreds of millions of years that followed, continental plates moved and the land was lifted up, creating huge pressure and heat, changing the deposits into the hard rocks we have today.

In more geologically recent times, a series of ice ages covered Britain, the last of which came to an end about 11,500 years ago. During these periods, huge sheets of ice built up over millennia, covering the land much as Greenland is today. Glaciers formed, where ice moves slowly downhill, its huge weight scraping away at the rock beneath, eroding the sandstone and exposing the underlying limestone, often forming U-shaped valleys. That is why the highest points in the Pennine Hills all have millstone grit as the bedrock which, being hard and insoluble, tends to be very stable.

As the climate warmed, ending the last Ice Age, forests thrived across the Pennines, including on the millstone grit heights. The continuous tree cover lasted until, at around six thousand years ago, the climate became cooler and wetter, causing water to collect on the impervious millstone grit rock. This inundated the tree roots so that forests gradually died out, the trees falling into the swamp where sphagnum mosses took over.

However, where the rain fell on limestone, the outcome was quite different. Limestone is formed largely of calcium carbonate which is sufficiently soluble in water for it to erode relatively easily. Where rivers flow, they cut deep valleys and, rather than accumulating on the surface, water seeps down through cracks in the rock, wearing it away until caves and potholes form. In the Yorkshire Dales, glacial action has exposed large areas of limestone, forming pavements, odd boulders and scars. Such features are known as 'karst' and lend the Yorkshire Dales their unique character.

The millstone grit and limestone bedrocks form the basis of strongly contrasting landscapes and habitats with very different flora and fauna. The result is the fascinating patchwork of wildlife habitats which are explored in this book.

A view to Ingleborough across the glacier-cut U-shaped Doe Valley in the Yorkshire Dales

Map of northern England showing the extent of the Pennines

CHAPTER ONE

Blanket Bog

The typical Pennine landscape is moorland, in which an open treeless carpet of low, rather uniform, vegetation stretches for miles into the distance. Over the upland heaths this may be the beige and green of tussocky moor grasses or the sombre green of heather which transforms into vivid purple as it flowers in the high summer. But higher up, on the ridges and sandstone plateaux where the land has been left to its own devices, blanket bog takes over and acres of moor grasses, heath and moss are dotted with dark pools and black walls of peat.

The ground here is soft and very boggy, comprising a deep layer of black peat that is mostly covered in vegetation, apart from where pools of water form in any depression or hollow or where the peat has been exposed. At such points, deep channels form between 'peat hags' which, combined with the bogs, make progress on foot arduous.

This is the landscape that inspired *Wuthering Heights* and *The Hound Of The Baskervilles*: universally bleak, often remote and occasionally dangerous. In the early days of the Pennine Way long-distance path, the hardships involved in crossing Kinder Scout, above the start at Edale, were legendary. In the official guide book, *The Pennine Way*, published in 1969, Tom Stephenson writes:

"Ahead, the ground is intersected with innumerable peat channels... into the boggy centre of Kinder where, except after prolonged drought, progress can be made only with some floundering from one less boggy patch to another." He goes on to describe *"...fissures sometimes 10 feet deep..."*

Peat bog is actually rather delicate as it is soft and bound together by a thin skin of mosses, bog grasses and cross-leaved heather. If this surface 'skin' is damaged then the peat begins to dry and break down, allowing water to start to flow, which causes rapid erosion. On Kinder and Bleaklow, huge expanses of bare peat and millstone grit were exposed following the Industrial Revolution, when rain which had been acidified by gases emitted by the factories below fell on the moors and killed the sphagnum moss from which peat is formed. Once exposed, streams could form which carried away the unprotected material. These bogs are jeopardised by installing drainage to benefit sheep and also by burning the heather to encourage grouse. This may seem to be no bad thing at first glance as blanket bog has no immediate commercial value, but they do have an importance.

The carbon reservoir

Peat has been used as fuel by humans for millennia and continues to be dug in parts of Britain and Ireland to keep the home fires burning. The energy in peat has been captured by photosynthesis, the process by which green plants turn atmospheric carbon dioxide (CO_2) into plant material, known as 'fixing' the carbon. This is how all green plants, including algae, bryophytes, ferns and flowering plants, grow and is the basis of the incredibly rich diversity of life on earth. When all or part of a plant dies, the remaining material is normally eaten, or rots away through fungal and bacterial action. As it decomposes,

Eroded Blanket bog on Kinder

CO_2 and/or methane (CH_4) are released back into the atmosphere to be taken up by another growing plant at some point. This is called the Carbon Cycle.

In the case of blanket bogs, the cycle is interrupted as the decomposition of plant material is halted by the anaerobic conditions that exist in the stagnant surface water so that partially degraded moss and other plant remains become trapped in the ground: this is the process of peat formation. Peat isn't only formed in the cool uplands, but anywhere on earth where plant material falls into oxygen-depleted water, such as the Siberian and Canadian tundra or waterlogged rainforests. The amount of carbon stored around the planet as partially rotted material and methane in bogs is vast and will only be released back into the atmosphere if it is exposed to the air. This happens if the covering vegetation is compromised or the surface is disturbed, which can allow the trapped methane to escape.

The process of the breakdown of peat and the release of the stored carbon has occurred through burning, exploitation for garden centres, draining and urban development. More insidious is the spontaneous decomposition of peat bogs, which happens when the peat dries out due to climate change, such as is happening in the Siberian lowlands. Although these problems apply to lowland bogs rather than upland blanket bogs, it is the case that peat bogs around the world represent a vast store of carbon in the form of solid carbon-rich material and of gaseous methane. So in these times when global warming resulting from atmospheric carbon is such a problem, their protection is critical if we are not to allow the situation to get a lot worse.

PLANTS OF THE BLANKET BOG

Pennine blanket bog is, by nature, low in nutrients and is acidic owing to the surface water and lack of oxygen in the peat which builds up because plant life does not decompose properly, so its nutrients are not released into the soil. Therefore the plants that thrive are specialists which like the wet, acidic conditions, and which can cope with the cool wet weather. Trees are scarce or non-existent, especially on the tops, so there is no cover or protection from the wind, apart from low-lying bog plants. This means that the animals inhabiting blanket peat bogs are specialists who can hide in the low vegetation and don't need to burrow, nor to roost in trees.

It is a harsh habitat where the combination of wind, rain, snow and generally low temperatures combine with a lack of nutrients to limit what thrives there and the speed of plant growth. The diversity of plant and animal species is quite limited but in the spring and summer a blanket bog can be vibrant with the white heads of cotton grasses bobbing in the breeze in the spring, purple heather in the summer and sweet autumn bilberries attracting a variety of birds.

SPHAGNUM MOSS

The plant that is most responsible for the accumulation of the peat which underlies the blanket bog is Sphagnum Moss, a few species of which cover much of the surface. It may be less noticeable than heather but it is ubiquitous on wet bogs to the extent that, in some places, the local moor is referred to as 'the moss'.

Mosses, like liverworts, are Bryophytes, which are more primitive than flowering plants and have very ancient origins. Their structure is comparatively simple being made up of filaments (rhizoids) that attach the moss to the

Below left: Hair moss
Below right: Feathery bog-moss

substrate and which can assist in water absorption, leaves which are only one cell thick arranged on a short stem. All parts of the plant, and especially the leaves, are very good at absorbing and retaining water, which is essential if they are to survive. However, being so small, they dry out easily and the sphagnum on Pennine blanket bog needs at least 1,200 mm (about 50 inches) of rainfall per year to thrive.

The sphagnum moss plant is, in fact, the green photosynthesising generation in its lifecycle, also known as the 'gametophyte'. The other generation is the 'sporophyte' which is produced on a stalk by the gametophyte, and produces reproductive spores which can be dispersed by the wind and have the potential to grow into new plants elsewhere.

Although sphagnum moss plants seem very delicate, their cell walls contain phenolic compounds which act as a preservative when the plant dies, so slowing or preventing the process of decomposition: this is the key to their peat-building properties. As sphagnum moss dies, the material is further prevented from decomposing by the low oxygen levels in the bog water so it simply sinks down to cover older material. Healthy peat builds by about 1mm each year which, over thousands of years, can amount to over 4 metres in depth in some Pennine locations.

A dozen sphagnum species can be found across the Pennines which can be identified, if required, using a smartphone app: to download it, search for MoorMOSS.

Restoration of damaged peat bogs

The law of unintended consequences tends to apply to most human activities when they impact on the natural world. The Industrial Revolution was powered by plentiful water from the Pennines, combined with coal mined from the extensive deposits, mostly found on the east side of the hills. Factories and towns spread across the Lancashire plain and the coal that they burned produced smoke which contained carbon dioxide and sulphur dioxide which combine with

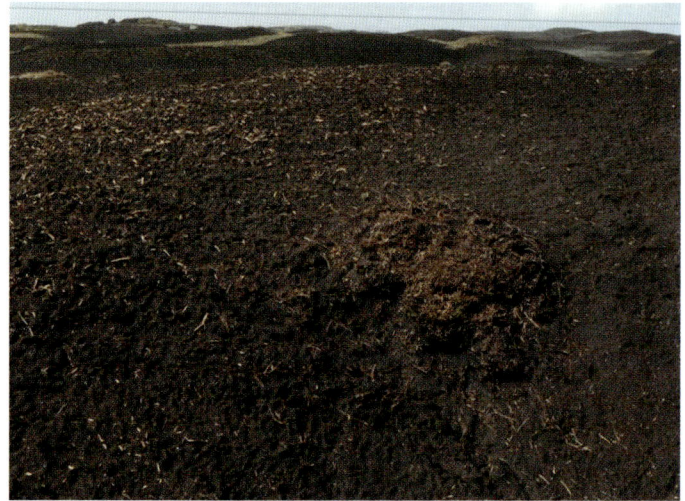

Above: Bare area of degraded bog land on Kinder Scout
Below: Restored blanket bog in the west Pennines

Hare's tail cotton grass

moisture in the atmosphere turning it acidic. This was then carried by the clouds that are blown over the Pennine uplands by the prevailing westerly winds and it fell as acid rain. At its peak in the mid 20th century, acid rain not only damaged people's health in the towns, but when it fell on the high moors, it acidified the standing water, killing the sphagnum moss and other plants, exposing bare peat from which water could run off much more easily.

With heavier rain storms in recent years, this has contributed to severe flooding of towns surrounding the hills, which has focused the minds of the UK governmental bodies on peat moor restoration. Projects are now underway along the length of the Pennines to sow mosses and the other bog plants on the exposed areas, restoring the peat bog habitats and slowing down the flow of water. Such improvements can be seen on Kinder Scout, Bleaklow, Bowland and the North Pennines.

FLOWERING PLANTS

Cotton grasses have unusual fibrous flowers which are characteristic of the moorland and brighten it up whilst often acting as a warning of wet bog. Cotton grasses are widely distributed across many cooler parts of the Northern Hemisphere up to the Arctic Circle, and three species grow in the Pennines. They are sedges rather than grasses, so the name is misleading as they are in a different plant family.

Common Cotton Grass (*Eriophorum angustifolium*) is quite a good indicator of where not to walk when rambling on the moors. It thrives in the wetter areas where the peat is very soft and feet can sink well above boot tops. It can be found growing in clumps, often covering the bog with its fluffy white flowers between June and September.

Cotton grass has dark green narrow leaves and from June onwards produces several flowers on each plant. It is less easy to distinguish from its surroundings in the

Common cotton grass

Hare's-tail cotton grass

Broad-leaved cotton grass

Hare's Tail Cotton Grass (*Eriophorum vaginatum*) is found on blanket bogs, but also copes with drier conditions. Its flowers have a single head and are less distinctive than the common species as the white pappi produced are much shorter. It forms tussocks that can carpet large areas of moorland and thrives in cold climates, being found across areas of tundra up to the Arctic circle.

Broad-leaved Cotton Grass (*E.latifolium*) has flat, yellow-green leaves and is found in the damper limestone meadows of Upper Teesdale and North Yorkshire only.

The Bogbean (*Menyanthes trifoliata*) also known as threefold or marsh trefoil, grows in and around pools and tarns where its three-lobed (trefoil) leaves poke up from the water, attached to long trailing stems below the surface. The five petals are usually pink on the outside and split into a spray of white tendrils or whiskers which can

Bogbean flower head

winter, when only the dull-green leaves are to be seen, but when it flowers in mid-summer, it is impossible to miss. Initially small flower heads develop with protruding white reproductive parts, but once fertilisation has taken place, hundreds of long 'pappi', or hairs, are produced which are used to carry the mature seeds on the wind. These fluffy seed heads resemble cotton but they can't be used for creating fabrics, although in the past they have been used for stuffing pillows.

look a bit like spun sugar. The plant can spread over acidic tarns and damp bogs, usually where the water is flowing rather than stagnant and it introduces a beguiling beauty in the springtime when it flowers. The fruits are shiny green pods containing large seeds.

Bogbean was so named as its leaves were said to resemble those of the broad bean, but it is not a legume (it is in the taxonomic order *Asterales*) and the name doesn't do it justice!

Bog Asphodel *(Narthecium ossifragum)* brings colour to the peat bogs when it produces its spikes of yellow star-like flowers in early summer. However its appearance warns of wet ground where you are likely to sink into the mire, as bog asphodel grows in the wettest places, especially where the water has some flow. It needs open, acidic conditions to thrive and won't tolerate shade nor dry conditions. Its nectar-rich flowers attract many insects throughout the summer until September, when the petals darken to deep orange. The flower spikes then turn reddish with pointed seed cases held by the sepals of each flower.

Bog asphodel is poisonous to sheep and cattle as it contains several toxins which cause a range of maladies including hepatitis, kidney failure and over-sensitivity to light.

The species name *ossifragum* means bone-breaker, which is derived from a belief that the plant also caused brittle bones in livestock. In fact this is brought about by the acidic conditions in bogs and a lack of calcium in the water and therefore in the plants being browsed, resulting in a nutritional deficiency.

Round-leaved Sundew *(Drosera rotundiflora)* is an insectivorous plant often found among the soggy sphagnum mosses on the wet peat and around pools. The plant compensates for its mineral-poor habitat by trapping and digesting insects, mostly midges. A small insect landing on one of the glistening drops which project from the leaf on many red stalks is held by the sticky fluid, and its struggles trigger the leaf to curl over slowly, enveloping the prey. The insect is then digested by enzymes and the nutrients

Bog asphodel in flower

are absorbed into the sundew. Thousands of midges are caught by each of these plants during the season.

The sundew produces small white flowers, but these often fail to open, and are self-pollinated in any case.

Round-leaved sundew

Cross leaved heath and moor grass on Derwent Edge in Derbyshire

HEATHER IN THE PENNINES

Three species of heather occur in the Pennines, often covering the landscape in dark-green foliage in the winter, then bringing vibrant colour to huge swathes of the fells in the summer.

Cross-leaved Heather *(Erica tetralix)* is the typical heather of the blanket bogs, thriving on the saturated surface where it is too wet for common heather. It grows in patches, usually mixed in with bog grasses and sphagnum, rather than in great swathes covering the landscape, as often occurs with ling. Its drooping flowers are paler pink than the other species and start to emerge in June, so it is the earliest to flower of the three species. The flowers hang in compact clusters at the ends of the plant's shoots whose leaves occur in whorls of four, thus its Latin name, *tetralix*. The plants have a slightly sticky feel owing to the secretions from glands on the leaves and sepals which help them cope with harsh winter winds and cold weather.

Common Heather *(Calluna vulgaris)* also known as ling has small flowers that are more dense than those on cross-leaved heather. Common heather is usually the plant that turns whole expanses of heath and moorland pink in August, when the concentration of millions of the tiny blossoms create a colourful blanket. Ling is tolerant to changing conditions, including some drying out, and even burning as part of managing moorland for grouse shooting.

Bell Heather (*Erica cinerea*) is the most colourful of the three with bright purple flowers which appear between July and September. It can form carpets of flowers, but does not like the wet bogs of the Pennine tops. Bell heather flowers are very rich in nectar so attract many pollinating insects including the rare bilberry bumblebee, that does not seem to visit ling. In the picture on page 24, bell heather is growing among dwarf gorse (*Ulex gallii*), which is also in flower.

The **Cloudberry** *(Rubus chamaemorus)* is a relative of the blackberry. Cloudberries are quite rare in Britain but common in the Baltic States and Scandinavia where its delicious salmon-pink berries are harvested. In Britain it occurs in the higher places and rarely sets fruit but does produce beautiful white rose-like flowers in the spring.

Right: Common heather flower close up
Below: Common heather in bloom in the Peak District

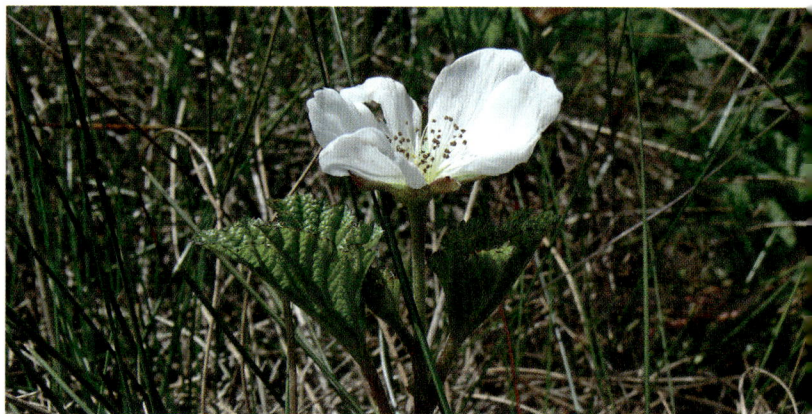

Above: Marsh thistle offering nectar to green-veined whites
Above right: Bell heather growing among dwarf gorse
Right: Cloudberry flower
Right below: Cloudberry fruiting

It can be found throughout the length of the Pennines, but only on the highest blanket bogs where the land rises above 600m.

It should not be surprising that the **Marsh Thistle** *(Cirsium palustre)* has green-veined butterflies enjoying its nectar-rich flowers: in fact, on the day that this photo was taken there were at least a dozen competing for them. Marsh thistle grows in damp places almost anywhere and is not a specialist of the blanket bogs, but you may well come across it and it is a good summer nectar source for insects. Marsh thistle is not welcome on the wet grazing meadows, where it can take over and is far too prickly for ruminants to eat.

Bog-rosemary *(Andromeda polifolia)* is a scattered dwarf shrub, quite rare in the Pennines but more abundant on lowland bogs in northern England. It has delicate, pink, flask-like flowers and narrow leathery leaves with a superficial resemblance to rosemary.

Bog-rosemary

The Labrador Tea Plant Conundrum

The name of the Labrador tea plant derives from the fact that in Labrador, the aromatic leaves were once used to make a hot drink. It occurs in just a handful of widely separated sites on the blanket bogs of the southern Pennines. It was cultivated in the UK from 1762 but was first found growing in the wild in Britain in 1860 and was dismissed as a garden escapee. However the remote and scattered blanket bog locations in which it does occur make this seem unlikely and further research has been carried out into its origins.

The species that occurs in the Pennines is *Ledum groenlandicum* which only occurs in Greenland and North America, whereas that under cultivation in Britain during the eighteenth century is likely to have been *Ledum palustre* which is abundant in Scandinavia and has distinctive narrow leaves. It is possible that Labrador tea arrived in the Pennines in the droppings of Greenland Wheatear, which eats seeds as well as insects, and flies directly from Greenland to Britain where it feeds on the high moors and bogs en route to its African wintering grounds. This has been deduced because most migrant birds from Greenland and Arctic Canada use Iceland as a staging post on their

way to Britain, but Labrador tea is notably absent from Iceland. Also the birds that do breed in Greenland (pink-footed goose, white-fronted goose, turnstone, dunlin) occupy coastal habitats and farmland rather than blanket bog in Britain. Because there are no other plants with a similar world distribution (Irish ladies' tresses – *Spiranthes romanzoffiana* – is the nearest) it seems likely that the seeds were transported naturally by birds, and greenland wheatear is the most likely candidate.

Labrador tea plant on Saddleworth Moor, and its flower head

Golden plover on a Peak District bog

BIRDS OF THE BLANKET BOG

There are two species of breeding birds which are specialists of the high blanket bogs, both of them waders: these are the golden plover *(Pluvialis apricaria)* and the dunlin *(Calidris alpina)*.

The **Golden Plover** *(Pluvialis apricaria)* arrives to lay claim to the best blanket bog territories as early as December, and if snow covers the moors they will descend to lower altitudes but return with the thaw. Their winter plumage is brown with small golden speckles on their wings and back, and fawn and white beneath on the breast. From the early spring, their plumage becomes more colourful and visible on the moors, as their belly turns black and their upper chest and throat become a tapestry of black, fawn and white triangles and diamonds. From this time, their melancholy whistle is heard across the moors.

Golden plovers have an unusual division of labour between the parents. Their nesting behaviour is interesting as, in the daytime, the female leaves the male on the nest to incubate eggs or brood young chicks, whilst roles are reversed at night when the male departs to the feeding-grounds. As a result they do their feeding in flocks comprised of a single sex, using separate locations. The young chicks feed on cranefly larvae (also known as leatherjackets) which are abundant on the wet blanket bog. When the youngsters start to grow, the parents may chaperone them over a mile of country to reach feeding pastures on nearby

Golden plover with cotton grass

A dunlin

farmland where they graduate to the more varied adult diet of craneflies, beetles and grasshoppers.

Flocks of golden plover fly to lowland fens and damp pastures for the winter months, where they often are joined by a winter influx from Scandinavia and gather in their hundreds or even thousands, usually accompanied by flocks of lapwings.

The **Dunlin** *(Calidris alpina)* is a much rarer breeding bird of the high blanket bogs and also less conspicuous. In winter dunlins are a plain brown and white bird but in summer their upper parts are richly patterned with orange and black, and the white belly is marked with a large, square black patch. Their song is a peculiar pulsating trilling which they emit both on the ground and while hovering in the air with dangling legs. However dunlin only sing during the early morning and late evening, when most humans have left the high tops, so few actually get to hear it.

Unlike golden plovers, the dunlin rarely leave the blanket bogs while nesting, feeding around the boggy pools on cranefly larvae. Their nesting habits are different too: the females will often fly off soon after the eggs have hatched, leaving the males to raise the chicks alone. Once the chicks can fly, the males depart, leaving groups of young dunlin to migrate together. Our British population of breeding dunlin is thought to winter mostly in Mauritania, but we currently have little evidence from recovered rings, and some are suspected of wintering in Britain.

The **Canada Goose** *(Branta canadensis)* is an introduced species which has become rather over-successful and is now found throughout the UK, including on the high bogs, where they have been known to breed. They have a distinctive white marking around the neck and a very loud honking call.

A curlew in flight

Non-breeding birds of the Blanket Bog

A number of other birds can be seen on blanket bogs in the Pennines, which are mostly at home on the lower grounds and which do not normally breed there.

The plaintive whistling call of the **Curlew** *(Numenius arquata)* is very much associated with wet, bleak places from the high Pennine tops to estuary wetlands throughout Britain. They are most likely to breed on lower moorland (see page 67) but they may be heard on the high bogs, particularly in the warmer months.

If you see a small mid-brown bird in the Pennines running between the grass tussocks and heather or which takes flight whilst calling a repeated 'seeep', it is likely to be a meadow pipit *(Anthus pratensis)*. They are frequently seen across the bogs, but breed on the drier grassy moors (see page 67).

Hen harriers and short-eared owl can breed on the bogs and can be seen hunting there for voles, although their normal breeding habitat is the heaths (see Chapter 2). Other occasional visitors include the cuckoo, lapwing, raven, merlin and buzzard.

MAMMALS & REPTILES OF THE BLANKET BOG

The waterlogged conditions on blanket bogs rule out animals that burrow underground, but foxes, badgers, weasels and stoats will all wander across this habitat. However the animals that live on blanket peat bogs must be able to hide in the low vegetation and not need to burrow or roost in trees and mustn't mind the cold, wet conditions so those that are resident are not specialists, but hardy individuals of species that occur widely in other parts of the country.

The **Field Vole** *(Microtus agrestis,* also known as short-tailed vole) are present in many blanket bog areas, but as it is one of the most common mammals in Europe, with a range extending from the Atlantic coast to Lake Baikal, it can't be regarded as a specialist. They feed on seeds, roots and leaves of whatever edible plant they can find and are an essential food source for many larger Pennine mammals, snakes and birds.

Field vole

A mountain hare on a gritstone outcrop

Even on the Pennine heights, the presence of winter snow is occasional rather than reliable and when absent, the hare's white winter coat ceases to work as camouflage, making the animal more obvious against the dark green foliage of the fells.

Adders *(Vipera berus)* are more common on the heaths, but they are found occasionally in the Pennine bogs. Their presence in this rather cool habitat will depend upon the availablity of prey species such as field voles, frogs and the eggs of ground-nesting birds such as the golden plover. They are a surprisingly hardy species for a reptile because their distribution ranges up towards the Arctic circle.

Frogs, and occasionally toads and smooth newts, can cope with the conditions, finding plenty of flies to eat. There are also plenty of fish-free pools in which to lay their spawn, although the acidity of the water can affect it adversely. The heather and tussock grass provide cover for amphibians to hide in, although they are still preyed on by birds.

Water voles *(Arvicola amphibius)* are to be found in a few blanket bog areas but are not common and are very difficult to spot. They have become quite rare in Britain and are more likely to be seen along river banks than on the high moors.

Mountain or **Blue Hares (***Lepus timidus)* occur in a restricted area of the Peak District but are much more widely spread in Scotland and Ireland, so are also known as the Irish Hare. The fossil record shows that they were present in Britain during the Ice Ages but subsequently disappeared from the country. The present population is descended from animals reintroduced for sporting purposes around 1870-1882 and they are now well-established in the Dark Peak moorlands.

Their diet is mainly heather, but they will eat grasses, rushes and almost any other plant that grows on the high moors.

The hare in this image was high on the blanket bog of the Peak District, seemingly unconcerned by a quiet human presence. The photo was taken in summer and its fur is brown, but turns white as winter approaches.

Adder, well camouflaged against dry bracken

Left: An adult male cranefly (Tipula paludosa)
Below: A water cricket
Right: A pondskater

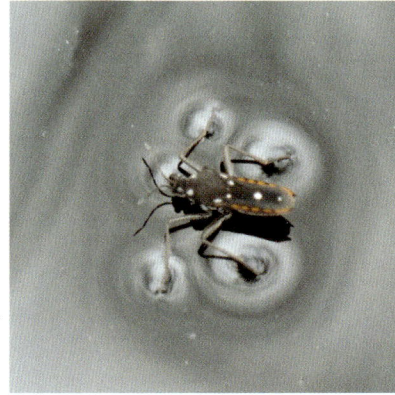

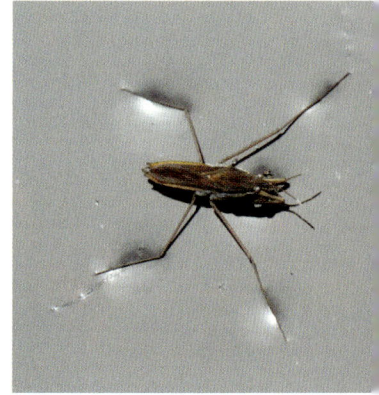

INVERTEBRATES OF THE BLANKET BOG

Blanket bogs are an important habitat for invertebrates such as flies, beetles and spiders, and these represent important food sources for an array of upland birds.

Craneflies

Craneflies and their larvae are one of the main food sources on the bogs for birds like dunlin, curlew and golden plover and provide sustenance for other visiting birds and amphibians. They are insects which are members of the family *Tipulidae*, in the true-flies order, or *Diptera*, which means 'two wings'. All dipteran flies have only one pair of wings, unlike dragonflies, and the hind wings are replaced by xylophone mallet-like balancing organs known as halteres (visible in the image). Tipulids have six long legs and a body that resembles the closely related mosquito (although no British tripulids bite humans). Craneflies are abundant on the moors, particularly in the autumn. They lay their eggs on damp ground or on water (depending on the species) which hatch into larvae known as 'leatherjackets'. These feed mostly on the roots of grasses and other plants, living underground and are present throughout the year. They are rich in protein so are sought after by animals which can dig them out from the soft, wet peat, particularly during the breeding season.

There are a few bugs that inhabit the blanket bog pools, preying on smaller invertebrates. These include the common **Pondskater** *(Gerris lacustris)* and the Caprai's **Water Cricket** *(Velia caprai)*, both of which skate on the water surface so are quite easy to spot. The water cricket's defence against predators is to exude nasty-tasting substances. Both insects are widespread and not upland specialists.

Dragonflies

Two specialist dragonflies can be abundant on high blanket bog, particularly if there are plenty of bog pools. The smaller of the two is the **Black Darter** *(Sympetrum danae)*, whose males are black all over whilst the females are a warmish yellow. They fly from July to September and beyond, feeding on smaller insects such as flies and midges which they grab as they dart about above the pools. Like all dragonflies, they fly in tandem during mating and males can remove the sperms from a previous mating so the male always holds on to his mated female until she has laid all of her eggs. So when people see dragonflies in tandem they might think they are mating, but they are more likely to be mate-guarding their own sperm. Eggs are laid among sphagnum at the pool edges and hatch in spring, when the larva develops among the mosses: black darters are unusual in that their larvae don't need to live in the water, but depend upon the layers of sphagnum to keep them moist.

The larger species of dragonfly is the **Common Hawker** *(Aeshna juncea)*, which is more rare and more localised than the related brown and southern hawkers. They are much larger and more active predators than the black darter and seldom land as they fly considerable distances over the moors in search of smaller insects. Females lay their eggs on aquatic plants in moorland pools where they remain until the following late spring. Development of the nymphs can take up to four years in these cool upland pools before an adult dragonfly emerges on warm days in the high summer.

Butterflies and moths

The only specialist blanket bog breeding butterfly is the rare **Large Heath** *(Coenonympha tullia)*, and across the Pennines it is only found in the Forest of Bowland, although populations also exist north of the Tyne Gap in the Northumberland fells. It is a true wetland species which can exist from sea level up to altitudes higher than its English range. The caterpillar takes a full year to develop, hibernating through the winter, and using hare's tail cottongrass for its main food. In the uplands, the adults

Black darter dragonfly

Common hawker male

emerge during June and July, with individuals surviving for a few days and feeding on cross-leaved heather nectar before laying eggs on the food plant.

Occasionally, other butterfly species will wander, or be wind-blown, up to the blanket bog from lower altitudes. These have no association with the habitat but will feed on the plants where nectar is available, as in the case of this green-veined white butterfly perched on a hare's tail cotton grass flower on a chilly morning.

A number of species of small moths are often seen among the grasses on the bogs, but most are quite plain and/or seem to disappear when they land as they fold their wings close over their backs, so no pattern is visible.

The **Common Heath Moth** (*Ematurga atomaria*) is a bit more noticeable, with its bands of brown and white or fawn on its wings which remain flat when it lands, so there is something to see. Even so, it easily disappears from view, being excellently camouflaged against the background. The male has feather antennae (below right) which the female (below left) lacks.

Left: Large heath butterfly on cross-leaved heather flowers
Above: Green-veined white on Hare's tail cotton grass
Below right: Male Common heath moth with its feathery antennae; and (below left) the female

PRESERVED FORESTS

Does this dead tree look a little incongruous in a tree-less landscape? It has been lost in time for about 5,000 years when the high moors of the Peak District were covered in forest, mainly oaks and Scots pines. Over the centuries, the climate became cooler and wetter and, on the flat plateau of the moors, water collected. Eventually the conditions became so poor that trees started dying and fell into the swampy ground in which sphagnum mosses were now thriving. Non-herbaceous material, such as tree trunks, are too big to rot to any extent in these low-oxygen conditions and can remain almost entire; preserved till eternity and buried beneath increasing depths of bog where there is no oxygen. Therefore, as further centuries passed, peat built up, enveloping the fallen tree wood and preserving it. It takes approximately 1,000 years for a metre of peat to be added, so today the remains of the preserved forest are buried under a peat blanket that can be over 4 metres in depth.

The preserved trees become visible if the peat is eroded away, particularly at the edge of the high plateau. The tree in the photograph lies along with many others at over 500 metres altitude, 200 metres above the valley floor, and has now started to decay, up to five millennia after it fell.

Places to find Blanket Bog habitats

Blanket bogs are found on the high tops of the Pennine Hills where the terrain is fairly level and these occur from the Dark Peak of Derbyshire up to the Tyne Gap. Kinder Scout is the best known bog in the south and is a typical high plateau. To the north of this, most of the higher areas are bog, including Bleaklow, Middle Edge Moss, Rushworth Moor and Langfield Common. The bog

Left: Ancient preserved wood on Alport Dale

continues between Hebden Bridge and Sutton-in-Craven. The Yorkshire Dales limestone interrupts the series, but plenty of bog is to be found north of Hawes and on up to the Tyne Gap.

Blanket Bog SSSIs

Name	Size (Ha)	OS Grid Ref	Location
Mallerstang Common	45,000	NY 804050	North Pennines
South Pennine Moors	21,000	SD 920300	Ilkley, Haworth & Moss Moors
West Nidderdale, Barden	13,500	SE 080705	Wharfedale to Nidderdale
Lovely Seat, Stainton Moor	10,100	SD 863933	Wensleydale to Swaledale

The Mystery of Will-o'-the-Wisp

Methane gas can be released through solid material and it sometimes rises to the surface of the bogs to be released into the atmosphere. Occasionally, escaping methane creates strange blue lights in the air above the bog surface known as 'Will-o'-the-wisps', 'jack-o'-lantern' or 'friar's lanterns'. They resemble flickering lamps which are said to recede if approached, drawing travellers from the safe paths and they have always been regarded as mysterious. Although people came to understand the cause of the lights, they remained enigmatic as no one could work out how the methane ignited in the damp bog atmosphere.

Researchers have recently discovered that a gas called diphosphane (P_2H_4) is often produced along with methane during partial decomposition of organic material and is known to burn spontaneously when it meets the air. Small amounts of this mixed in with the released methane are sufficient to ignite the mixture, causing the strange bluish will-o'-the-wisp lights, solving the slightly sinister mystery.

Sunset over a blanket bog

CHAPTER TWO
Upland Heaths

Upland heaths are probably the best-known landscape in the Pennines as they are more accessible than blanket bogs and occur along the entire Pennine chain. These two habitats form the landscape that we think of as 'moorland', where huge swathes of heather and bilberry rise and fall like an endless carpet until they meet the open sky. In the Pennines, the drystone-walled fields start to become more difficult to manage from about 250m altitude as a result of the cool temperatures and high rainfall, which leaches nutrients from the soil. In many places, smaller, actively managed fields tend to get larger and more heath-like above 300 metres, and upland heath will be seen where land is not drained and fertilised. Between 350 and 450 metres, the land becomes too marginal to be worth farming, so the walled fields tend to peter out and true moorland starts, where the land is open and unenclosed. Much of the Pennine landscape, where it isn't too wet and boggy, will fall into the upland heath classification. Blanket bog predominates above this (and often at lower altitudes) as the bedrock is usually millstone grit on which water collects,

Above: Common heather (Calluna) in flower among the gritstone rocks of the high moors

Previous page: Hallam Moor near Sheffield with Stanedge Lodge among the purple heather

particularly where the land is level (see Chapter 1). Heath is drier, usually because it is on a slope where water can run off, and sphagnum can't accumulate into deep layers of peat. At the very highest points in the Pennines, such as at the 893 metre summit of Cross Fell, the habitat is classed as alpine: in other words, mountain. Here the climate is even harsher and plant growth is limited such that the surface is almost bare rock.

In this chapter, the typical natural history of Pennine upland heaths is discussed, which is more diverse than blanket bog.

Natural England defines blanket bog as where the peat depth is greater than 40cm and their interactive website map (www.natureonthemap.naturalengland.org. uk/MagicMap.aspx) implies that it covers more area than upland heath. The reality on the ground is more complex than that as the two habitats merge into each other and can change due to land use, for instance if drained. You will usually know if you are in blanket bog as your feet will be on soft, wet peat whereas upland heaths are normally drier and covered in common heather or moor grasses, rather than cross-leaved heather.

In its natural state, heath is populated by a variety of dwarf shrubs including common and bell heather, bilberry, crowberry and cowberry, often in a mosaic with patches of grassland, bracken or woodland, particularly near the moorland edge. Sadly, it is often the case that intensive moorland management destroys this diversity and leads to domination by a single species, usually heather, purple moor-grass or bracken. The prevalence of common heather encourages the presence of red grouse and has the benefit of turning the dark green moor into a sea of mauve in the high summer that almost shines where the sunlight breaks through.

Bilberry is the other main shrub that can cover extensive areas of heath, usually where grazing is not taking place, so it is often found where the ground is rough and boulder-strewn. Where moor grasses dominate, the heaths are less colourful and diverse, as the grasses have poorer food value and offer less cover than heather and bilberry.

Trees, particularly birch, often form copses on the heaths, some merging into woodland. In such places the number of animal species present is likely to increase dramatically as the trees offer refuge, nesting sites and a greater diversity of food for birds and mammals. Although our concept of heath or moorland is treeless, it is kept that way through grazing and burning: left to itself it is likely that large areas would become scrub or woodland.

Although a moor can seem like a wild place, almost

all land in the Pennines is managed to some degree, even the blanket bog. Quite a lot of today's heaths, particularly where the land is less sloping, is actually drained bog where drainage ditches have been dug and are maintained to take water away. Coming full circle, in some places the peat bog is being restored, and the gullies and ditches are blocked or filled in so that the soil becomes saturated and sphagnum moss can grow once more.

The 17th century philosopher John Locke wrote: *"Yet by the labour of his body and the work of his hands…whatsoever then he removes out the state that nature has provided…he has mixed his labour with, and joined to it something that is his own, and thereby makes it is property…."*. This concept of gaining ownership of land through 'improving' it, remains with us today. 'Improving' land for agriculture or development almost always results in the loss and/or destruction of

Whitwell Moor, South Yorkshire, in the foreground where bilberry mixes with heather on the moor, which forms a patchwork with farmland and forest. Barnside Moor in the distance is covered in flowering heather

wildlife, whose value, or natural capital, is discounted. The idea that wild places, places that are naturally open and bleak, are 'wastelands' still has currency, particularly with urban populations. So it is that conservationists are forever on the back foot, being presented with the argument that a balance is needed between conservation and exploitation, and each time a little more land is lost to development.

Prompted by the loss of natural habitats and mismanagement of the countryside, there is now a movement demanding the 'rewilding' of the countryside; that is, allowing nature to take its course, reverting land to a more natural state.

The tension between those who wish to manage the moors for financial gain, through grouse shoots or livestock farming, and those who want a wild unmanaged landscape, creates heated debate. There is even tension between those managing the moors for the benefit of a particular rare species of habitat and rewilding purists who believe that they should be left entirely alone. In recent times, the rewilding cause has found some political support because of heavy rain running off the hills and flooding towns below: a dry, burned moor holds far less water than a natural landscape of trees, shrubs and bog.

Wessenden Valley which is an extensive white moor

THE IMPACT OF MOORLAND MANAGEMENT

There are few parts of England that have not been altered by human activity, and that includes the Pennines. Forests once covered a good proportion of these hills but, where they hadn't been lost through a changing climate, they were chopped down for fuel or land clearance. Over the centuries a lot of wild moor has been 'tamed' to feed the demand for land and to provide opportunities to make a living from it, particularly through farming but also for country sports and stone or mineral extraction. These have wrought enormous changes in the landscape and resulted in wildlife and plant communities having to adapt or die out, to be replaced by other species that are better suited to the new conditions.

Such change has often been government funded, such as the 20th century programme to drain the moors in an attempt to enhance their commercial potential through grazing or planting forests of fast-growing conifers. This process is now being reversed through a number of projects in the Pennines and elsewhere which are attempting to restore the carbon-saving peat by returning the land to

Above: The moors of Upper Teesdale

blanket bog and also to remove single-species conifer plantations and replace them with native broad-leaved woodland. (www.moorsforthefuture.org.uk)

Another commercial use of large stretches of moorland is grouse shooting which usually involves patch burning of heather and the control of predators.

Grouse Shooting

One of the country sports whose growth in popularity and management practices have had a huge impact on the Pennine upland heaths is grouse shooting. The quarry is the native red grouse: a bird that is a specialist of the heather moors and one that is not reared in captivity. It has several attractions as a quarry. Firstly, it is faithful to its moorland habitats and will defend a territory for much of the year, whereas in contrast, the black grouse is more wide-ranging across a large area and a range of different habitats. Secondly, it is the fastest flyer among game birds, providing a challenge for the guns. And finally, it is reputed to be the tastiest of game birds so is valued by restaurants and in dining rooms.

Grouse shooting has grown to become an important revenue source for some landowners and accessible by anyone who has the right connections and is willing to pay the rate for a day's shooting. As the number of places available on grouse shoots is limited, the fees tend to be high, which brings money into these rural areas. Shooting provides employment in the countryside and it attracts visitors to the area, so is an activity that has a wider commercial value where it takes place.

As with any human activity, the size and extent of attendant problems depends upon the numbers of people taking part, the intensity with which the land is managed, and the resources required to facilitate their enjoyment. In the case of grouse shooting, the moor is

Above: Burning the heather in the South Pennines
Below left: Tray of medicated grit for grouse, to prevent a parasitic threadworm. Below right: A sunken grouse shooting butt with a pattern of intense burning in the distance

Red grouse in the heather

managed so as to artificially raise the number of birds above that which would be supported if nature took its course, and this has implications for other wildlife. Impacts on the landscape include the building of access roads and shooting butts, and the regular burning of heather in blocks, creating a sort of chequerboard appearance on the moors.

A heather moor is the main habitat of the red grouse, providing insects and tender shoots that their chicks need to eat, although they can also find food on wetter boggy areas. The young thrive best when the heather is short as they are too small to move through mature heather with its jungle of woody stems or to reach food sources when the heather is fully grown. In order to provide a plentiful supply of food and to maximise the number of chicks in an area, the heather is burnt on a rotating basis, creating a patchwork of short and longer vegetation. The practice has been carried out for more than a century, but is intensifying as shoots grow and become more commercial.

As the red grouse is a native bird and it is being encouraged to prosper in its natural habitat, the management of moors for grouse shooting could be seen as a benign countryside activity that contributes to the prosperity of the area. It also provides a reason to conserve

A series of numbered shooting butts going up Foulstone Moor above Strines

heather moorland and burning the heather provides a varied habitat for other birds. It is claimed that populations of golden plover, curlew and lapwing can increase on grouse moors, at least in the short term.

However, as tends to be the case when humans exploit the countryside, there is a down-side. In many cases, wet moors are drained so that the heather grows better and, as has been described in Chapter 1, that will have a negative effect on peat, which has its own value as a carbon sink and absorber of water. It also kills off sphagnum mosses and may change the acidity of the ground water, altering the entire ecosystem.

Burning the heather in blocks often gives the moor a geometric 'chequerboard' appearance, which is very different from its natural state. It also results in the demise of many leatherjackets, the larval stage of craneflies and a very important food source for moorland birds, including those mentioned above. Heather burning has a destructive effect on the soil structure and endangers amphibians and ground-dwelling invertebrates which make up a healthy ecosystem. In other words, such moors can become depleted in biodiversity over the medium and long term. For instance, studies have found that an increase in moorland birds following heather burning can reverse so that numbers are drastically down after 20 years of such management.

Gamekeepers routinely kill predators such as foxes, stoats, weasels and crows within the law as a means of ensuring a harvestable surplus of grouse. This benefits other ground-nesting birds but it creates an imbalanced ecosystem. There is also growing evidence that legally protected birds of prey, including raptors and owls are being removed. Raptors are protected by the Wildlife and Countryside Act 1981, but they have historically been regarded as pests by gamekeepers. The reality is that today, the hen harrier is close to extinction as a breeding bird across the Pennines as well as nationwide and an often heated debate between landowners and conservation bodies continues.

One further problem with intensive grouse moor management is that, where grouse population densities are higher than normal, diseases and parasites become a problem, and in particular a nematode worm *Trichostrongylus tenuis*. When infected droppings have been left among the heather, the nematode eggs therein hatch into larvae which move up the plants and are ingested by the birds as they feed. The high density of birds means that grouse can become heavily infested with worms which makes them listless and reluctant to fly. To counter this problem gamekeepers put out large amounts of grit, which the grouse need to ingest to help with digestion, medicated with fenbendazole to kill the worms in the birds' guts. As with many solutions, the medicine used to deal with gut worms in grouse, or any livestock, creates a problem for the ecology, as they also damage or kill many naturally-occurring invertebrates.

In summary, a grouse moor is certainly not a natural habitat for wildlife, but neither are many nature reserves, which are managed to support particular species. Shooting serves a demand for the sport and contributes to the local economy. Heather burning increases the structural diversity of the moor which can help the lapwing and plover as well as the grouse, at least over the short term, but is likely to have a longer-term deleterious effect on wildlife. Intense management affects the hydrology of the moor negatively, can be unsightly and creates an unbalanced and unsustainable ecosystem, but one which many in the countryside fight to retain. It is a scenario for an often polarised debate.

LIVESTOCK FARMING IN THE UPLAND HEATHS

Livestock have been put out to graze on the moors for centuries and ancient pens, walls and ruins can be seen in many high places along the Pennines.

Across most of the Pennine heaths, agricultural practices continue to define the landscape and the type of ecosystem. Upland farms almost all run sheep, which crop the softer grasses and young shrub growth close to the ground, but they don't eat the harder, more fibrous moorland plants, such as mat grass. The climate is harsh and nothing grows in the winter, so traditionally, animals were taken off the hills as the days shortened and moved to lower pastures where they were fed on hay that was grown on local hay meadows. There they would remain until spring growth was once more available on the moors. If sheep numbers are kept under control, this form of hill farming

An ancient sheep pen ruin

can be quite sustainable with limited adverse effects on the moorland ecosystem, although the development of scrub and trees is very limited.

However, the paucity of grazing and the fragility of ecosystems on the Pennine fells mean that upland farming has to be carefully managed if damage to landscape and biodiversity is to be avoided. As with grouse shoots, a great deal depends upon the extent and intensity of management.

Moors that contain a patchwork of habitats are particularly good for wildlife, where heather moor, low-lying blanket bog and small patches of grass and woodland merge into each other. Biodiversity in any area is strongly affected by the nature of the dominant vegetation. For instance, where the bilberry is common it provides food and cover for birds and other small animals. However, if grazing pressure is too heavy, particularly during winter, the shrubs will give way to coarse grasses like purple moor grass which the sheep prefer not to eat, resulting in the accumulation of a mass of dead grass. Moors that are covered in these grasses are known as 'white moors' and are likely to be poor in wildlife, including the red grouse.

Over-grazing in high places is a major cause of habitat and ecosystem degradation such that the UK Biodiversity Action Plan published by Defra in 2016 says:

"It has also been estimated that 440,000ha of land in the uplands in England and Wales have less than 25% cover of heather (i.e. grassland containing suppressed dwarf shrubs). There is likely to be further significant loss of heather moorland to acid grassland if current grazing levels and pressures continue."

This is hardly new, but since 1980, when European Union agricultural policies were changed, subsidies have tended to increase the problem. The change to paying farmers according to the number of sheep they owned (so-called 'headage' payments) caused numbers of sheep on the hills to increase by 50% between 1980 and 1992. As farmers increased the size of their flocks to gain income, they found ways to get more grazing out of the moors, which became overstocked. Far more sheep were kept on the moor throughout the winter, their diet supplemented by silage at feeding stations in place of hay, which in turn resulted in the loss of hay meadows as they were turned to silage production. Meanwhile grazing sheep prefer moorland shrubs, like bilberry, to coarse moorland grasses, resulting in the further spread of white moor.

In the springtime, purple moor grass produces new shoots, known as 'spring bite', which sheep can eat, but these are obscured by the fibrous mat of dead material. For many farmers, the solution is to burn the white moors during the winter so that the mat of old growth is removed and the new growth becomes immediately available for grazing. This takes the pressure off the other species as the sheep

Left: Sheep on grass heath

congregate on the burnt areas to feed, but this is not the end of the story. The sheep drop large amounts of dung onto these burnt moors which fertilises the ground and promotes the more vigorous growth of the purple moor grass and bracken, which can colonise an area very rapidly and is difficult to control. The resultant landscape is thus radically altered as bilberry, heather and other moorland plants are replaced by unpalatable bracken and white grasses.

Finding a balance

Grazing by cattle or sheep is frequently introduced to heath- and grass-land wildlife reserves in order to control the growth of scrub and woodland, preserving the open habitat and promoting biodiversity. So limited grazing has definite benefits for the upland heaths of the Pennines, although great care has to be taken regarding the type of animals used. For instance, cattle are usually kept out of water catchments because of the increased risk of water contamination by organisms such as cryptosporidium.

Farmers work very hard for modest incomes to conserve the hills that they love whilst earning a living through hill sheep farming. However, the long-term effects of any change to farming practices, particularly where livestock numbers and range are increased, only unfold gradually, but can end up being severe. Few people welcome walking or driving through mile after mile of monochrome white moor where birds are absent or walking through endless tussocks of molinia.

There is an argument that sheep farming should be phased out as it is unprofitable and damages the ecosystem. Some also attest that taking sheep off the hills would enhance flood protection of the valleys below through the growth of more diverse vegetation that would slow the flow of water following heavy rainfall. Whilst this 'rewilding' argument has many attractions for some nature conservationists, it causes deep disquiet among

A sheep paddock on marginal land above Whaw in Arkengarthdale, North Yorkshire

communities where hill farming is seen as an honourable occupation which is at the core of local values: this is a scenario ripe for unproductive conflict between two sides, both of whom love the countryside.

Central government is going to be the main driver either way, as subsidies have a powerful effect on farming practices. A decision on whether hill sheep farming should be encouraged or discouraged should take into account its sustainability and financial viability along with the nation's priorities for its wildlife and landscape. Human civilization has developed through taking unproductive land, or 'wasteland', and turning it into something that has utility, usually without regard for the natural capital it holds. As we learn more about how endangered natural habitats and wildlife are, and the true value of natural capital, that approach is being challenged. We can only hope that people work together, looking for common objectives and solving problems in a cooperative spirit, or the path to a new, more cautious, attitude to the use of our countryside is fraught with obstacles and the potential for conflict.

A Hen harrier in flight

WILDLIFE IN THE UPLAND HEATHS

Because the upland heath presents such a varied habitat, so the species likely to be encountered depend on whether you are in a wide open heather moor, in a boggy dip, or in a mixed 'patchwork' area.

In the winter, you are likely to see grouse, but could encounter golden plover and mountain hares. Pink-footed geese are a frequent winter sight, as they fly in great skeins between Lancashire and the east coast. However, most of the summer migrant birds such as whinchat, wheatear and ring ouzel migrate to Africa for the winter, often fuelling up on moorland berries before they go.

A few residents like the stonechat and wren tough it out, but suffer great losses in harsh winters, so to avoid this, some birds (and mammals) descend to lower altitudes in winter, returning in the spring.

So the upland heaths in winter can be spectacular, but the best time to see wildlife starts in the spring, when buds swell, the migrants return and the annual mating rituals get underway.

In this chapter we will explore the typical plants, invertebrates, birds and mammals of the upland heaths and describe some of their habits and where they are to be found. A visitor to a moor may also encounter species such as thrushes, wheatears, wood pigeons or gulls from the valleys below, which are there in search of food. Which species will be present at any one time is unpredictable and depends on the amount of disturbance, the weather and the whims of nature, but if one remains quiet and unobtrusive, the chances of seeing something interesting will be greatly improved.

DOMINANT UPLAND HEATH COVER PLANTS

Common heather is the defining plant of the heather moors and the most important food plant for at least 40 species of insect as well as the red grouse. Left to its own devices, heather can grow to 60cm or more in height and form a dense carpet canopy over large areas, but it can also be found interspersed with patches of bell heather, bilberry and moor grasses. Moor grasses are an important component of the

upland bogs and heaths and the three most common are all acid-loving and lime-hating (calcifuge) plants that grow in tufts, or clumps and thrive in nutrient-poor conditions.

Purple Moor Grass (*Molinia caerulea*) is so-called because its flower spikes have a purplish hue especially in sunlight. Its rough-textured leaves are quite broad and have a bluey-green tint. It grows in wet moorlands and forms large, ankle-breaking tussocks which are difficult to walk through. Because the grass is so unpalatable, the tussocks are often covered in a thick blanket of dead grass which the farmers burn off to give sheep access to fresh growing shoots for the sheep to eat. The tussocks survive annual burning and, fertilised by sheep droppings, often come to dominate large areas of moorland.

Above: Heavily-grazed moor, now degraded to mat grass and moss
Below: Purple moor grass

Below: A 'white moor' in early spring, completely dominated by purple moor grass

Above left: Wavy hair grass flower head
Above centre: Mat grass plant
Above right: Sheep's fescue at Meltham
Below: Bilberries
Below right: Crowberries

Wavy Hair Grass *(Deschampsia flexuosa)* is very common on untended areas around Britain and so named because of its flowers, which are on long thin stems with wispy flowerheads. It can grow in very nutrient-poor conditions and thin soils and is good at colonising the edges of bare rock. It has a purplish flowering stem which rises higher than the leaves, creating a mist-like appearance over the ground.

Mat Grass *(Nardus stricta)* is a much shorter, narrow-leaved grass that tends to form a dense mat of fibrous dead plant material which contains silica, so is somewhat inedible. It grows in drier places than purple moor grass, right up to the highest areas.

Other non-specialist grasses colonise upland heaths, including common bent *(Agrostis capillaris)* and **Sheep's Fescue** *(Festuca ovina)*. Sheep's fescue is short, upland grass that forms small tussocks in drier areas and is the main larval food plant of the small heath butterfly in the uplands.

Bilberry *(Vaccinium myrtillus)*. Like heather, the bilberry likes acid soils and can dominate large areas of Pennine moorlands, although it is not usually as widespread as common heather and is most concentrated in the north-western areas. It normally grows to about 50cm in height and forms a spreading canopy that can be quite dense, but less difficult to walk through than heather, with which it will often be mixed.

The bilberry is a valuable food plant for many heathland residents. In the springtime, green hairstreak butterflies can often be found fluttering over the plants or taking a rest on a leaf. Its clusters of dark purple berries are rich in sugars and vitamins so are an important food source in the lead-up to winter, attracting birds from far and near. However, where there are sheep, the tender spring growth and flowers tend to get eaten so there are no berries, so the best places to find bilberries will be road verges or fenced-off reserves where sheep cannot go.

Right: Cowberry with crowberry and some bilberry in the background

Other Heathland Plants

Crowberry *(Empetrum nigrum)* is one of the moorland shrubs which is in the family *Ericaceae*, so closely related to the heathers. It is evergreen with a low, sprawling habit comprised of reddish-brown stems bearing many narrow, pointed leaves. It produces tiny purple flowers in the spring and spherical, black berries from May right through the summer and into autumn. The berries are edible but rather tasteless and, unlike bilberries, they contain only small amounts of vitamins.

Because of its spreading habit, crowberry is good for stabilising the surface of exposed peat, so is a useful plant in moorland and bog regeneration.

Cowberry *(Vaccinium vitis-idaea)* is a dwarf evergreen shrub with thick, leathery leaves which is a close relative of the bilberry. It is found most typically in moorland but does not thrive when the moors are burnt, so tends to be less common than heather or bilberry. It bears white or pink bell-shaped flowers in clusters from June and edible, but sharp-tasting red berries.

Above: Deer grass
Below: Heath bedstraw

Rosebay willowherb

Deer Grass or **Deer Sedge** *(Trichophorum cespitosum)* is not a grass, but a sedge producing dense growth of smooth stems which are vibrant green and topped with a terminal brown flower. It is not particularly common in the Pennines but is most at home on wet moors and the edge of blanket bog.

Heath Bedstraw *(Galium saxatile)* is found on heaths throughout Britain and is a very common herb on acidic heaths and moors. It spreads across the ground and can form dense mats or cushions, producing small white flowers on short upright stems in the summer.

Rosebay Willowherb *(Chamerion angustifolium)* is a native plant which is found on waste ground, embankments, rocky places, mountain scree and open woodland throughout Britain. It is one of the first plants to colonise a barren area, such as after burning, so is known as 'fireweed' in America. Its rhizomes enable it to form dense clumps which bring spectacular colour to parts of the Pennines in the high summer as the tall stems are crowned with clumps of pink flowers.

It is nectar rich and also has several medicinal properties valued by herbalists.

Above: Water avens swathe above Wensleydale
Below: Water avens flowers

Water Avens *(Geum rivale)* is a plant of northern Britain which grows in marshes, wet meadows and hedge banks. It has lantern–like flowers with crimson sepals over delicate pink or apricot petals which develop into round seed heads with projecting filaments all over. It can take over extensive pieces of ground, but needs to be looked at quite closely to appreciate its beauty.

UPLAND HEATH FERNS

Bracken *(Pteridium aquilinum)* is the most familiar of the moorland ferns and it can cover large areas, spreading if the moor is subject to burning and grazing. Bracken spreads quickly by underground rhizomes and can grow to over human head height, so dominates all other non-woody plants. It also produces countless spores on the underside of its fronds which are blown great distances by the wind. This ability to expand rapidly is at the expense of other plants and wildlife, and can cause major problems for land users and managers which requires good management to limit its spread.

It dies back in winter but its fibrous stem builds up to form a layer of dry brown litter that is often used for nesting by the small upland birds, such as twite, whinchat and meadow pipit.

Broad Buckler Fern *(Dryopteris dilatata)* is also quite common but not as ubiquitous as bracken. It grows in a wide range of habitats occurring on open moorland, road verges and in shady places such as forest floors. Its fronds are three-pinnate which gives them a rather light and elegant appearance. Its stem has a brown beard and a dark brown central structure.

Hard Fern *(Blechnum spicant)* grows in shady places, often in woods but also out on the moors. It has two types

Lemon-scented fern   Fir clubmoss

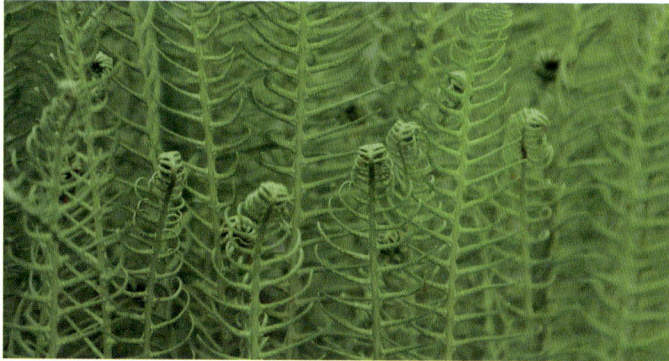

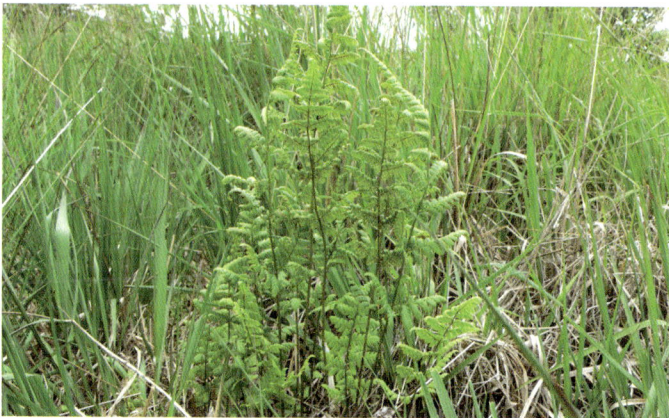

Left: Hard fern
Middle: Lemon-scented fern
Bottom: Narrow buckler fern
Right: Scaly male fern on a roadside

of frond, or leaf, one of which is sterile and the other is reproductive. The sterile leaves are more distinctive, with flat, wavy-margined leaflets 5-8mm wide, while the fertile leaves have much narrower leaflets, looking more like a step-ladder and each with two thick rows of spore-bearing sori on the underside.

Lemon-Scented Fern (*Oreopteris limbosperma*) is an inconspicuous fern that grows in tufts to about 120cm height in wetter places. It is a late developer and its fronds can still be seen unfurling while most other ferns are already fully out. The name comes from the lemon aroma which is released when its leaves are crushed.

Narrow Buckler Fern (*Dryopteris carthusiana*) often grows in wet moorland flushes but is not easy to identify as it is very similar to the much more common broad buckler fern and both favour damp places, although the broad species tends to prefer woodland settings. Botanists look at the brown scales on the stem to be certain as broad buckler has a dark centre whereas narrow buckler has uniform coloured scales. The fronds do not grow from a central crown, but rise up sporadically from the underground rhizomes.

Fir Clubmoss (*Huperzia selago*) is a very small descendent of the first vascular plants that evolved, over 400 million years ago. Plants from the same family were trees, which grew in great forests during the Carboniferous period. The fir clubmoss grows as a group of stems, each rarely reaching over 10cm in height and covered in a spiral of soft pointed leaves. It is not particularly common, but is found on the highest ground over the length of the Pennines.

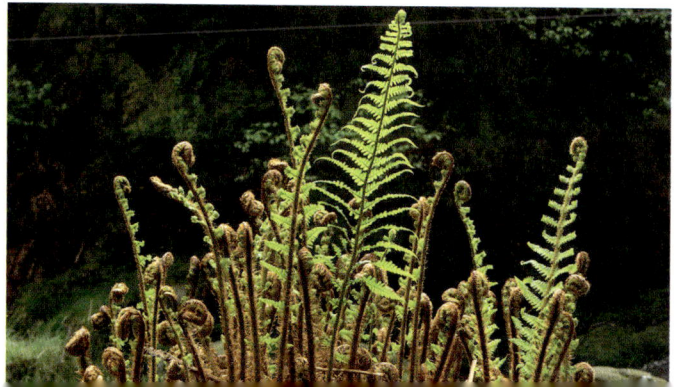

BRYOPHYTES AND LICHENS

Some wetter upland heaths are particularly rich in lichens, liverworts and mosses, including sphagnum, although not normally where burning takes place. Bryophytes are simple plants which cannot cope with drying out so are mostly found in damp and sheltered areas but mosses can also cover large areas of open fell, particularly when they have been damaged. Liverworts are almost always found around standing or flowing water.

Lichens are found coating most upland rock outcrops as well as producing sometimes spectacular displays on tree trunks and branches. They are a symbiotic relationship between fungi and algae which enables them to grow in very harsh conditions, but many are very sensitive to air pollution and acid rain, and they will not survive fire.

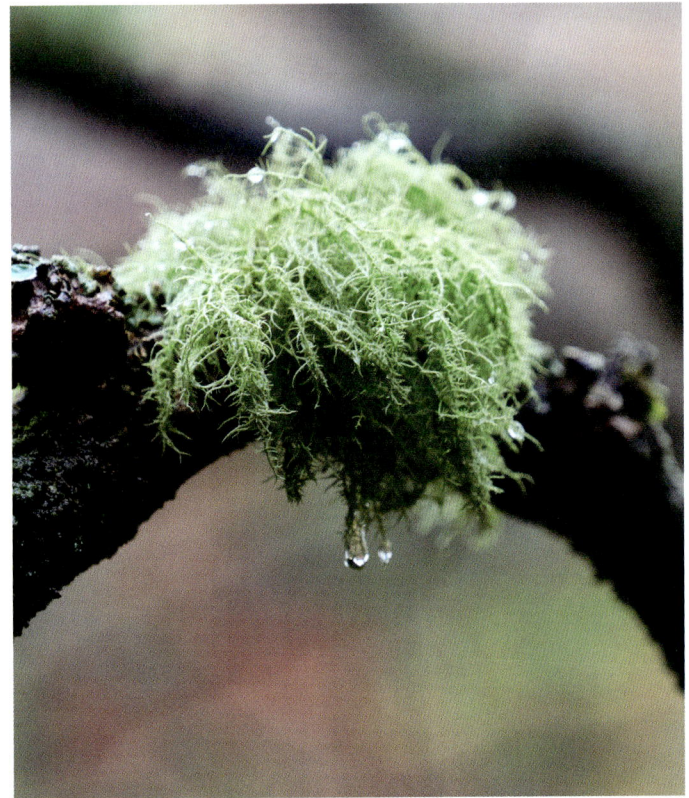

Above: Lichens on a tree branch above Langsett, West Yorkshire

Left: Mosses and hart's tongue fern on Froggatt Edge, Derbyshire

Right: Mosses covering a wall and tree stump in the Ingleborough National Nature Reserve

INVERTEBRATES OF THE UPLAND HEATHS

Upland heaths in the Pennines support a wide range of invertebrates which are the principle food source for frogs, toads, and many of the birds. Few of them are obvious to the casual observer or walker as they are small and inconspicuous and most commonly in pools, or under rocks and among moorland vegetation. In the colder months, it is likely that none will be seen, but as the air warms, bumblebees, dragonflies and butterflies take flight in the better weather. Only these more visible and significant invertebrates are described here as one has to be something of a specialist to find and study the many small, hidden beetles, flies and spiders.

BUTTERFLIES

Although the climate of the Pennine hills is cool and damp, they are frequented by butterflies, some of which can be regarded as heathland species. The Pennines also attract visitor butterflies, tempted to the moors by the abundance of nectar.

Butterflies lay their eggs during the warmer months and these normally hatch into the larval caterpillar stage within a few days or weeks. There may be two or three broods in a good year. The caterpillars eat voraciously, unless they emerge in the autumn, when they may over-winter and hibernate during cold weather, before pupating as a chrysalis. During the chrysalis stage, the insect is completely defenceless, so the chrysalis usually has to be well camouflaged and hidden from view. The adult, or imago, is the butterfly, and its main purpose is to mate and lay eggs.

The butterflies whose entire lifecycle takes place in the Pennine uplands need to be able to cope with the cool damp weather and long winters.

Small Heath (*Coenonympha pamphilus*). This tiny orange and brown butterfly inhabits grassy moorlands throughout the Pennines where its caterpillars feed on the finer grasses, such as sheep's fescue. Like the green hairstreak, it never basks with its wings open so a marbled grey hindwing is all you will see when it is resting. The forewing is orange, with an eyespot towards the tip that comes into view at the first hint of danger. This eyespot deflects attention away from the vulnerable body, giving the butterfly chance to escape with just a little wing damage if a bird's peck is misdirected. Again, they are hard to find when at rest, being small and camouflaged, and not that easy to follow in flight, but if you manage to follow one, they do tend to stop and rest frequently.

Small heath

Small copper

Small Copper *(Lycaena phlaeas)*. This pretty little butterfly is also widely spread and not a heathland specialist, but it can be found on the Pennines almost anywhere on a warm summer's day if you are lucky. It will seek out sheep's sorrel (*Rumex acetosella*) on which to lay its eggs: this plant often colonises bare ground such as path edges, eroded areas and recent moor burns.

Green Hairstreak (*Callophrys rubi*). This little butterfly can be easily passed by unnoticed as it is very well-camouflaged against green foliage, but it is worth looking out for as its green underwings, made up of shiny scales, are quite lovely. These green scales are unique among British species: although the green-veined white and orange tip butterflies appear to have green on the wings, this is brought about by a combination of black and yellow scales whose combined effect deceives the human eye. The green hairstreak occurs on lowland grasslands and heaths but is also probably the most common butterfly living in the Pennines where it lays its eggs on bilberry. It lives in groups or colonies in sheltered places where bilberry abounds, although its presence is hard to predict in any location. It flies in abundance in the Pennines in May, seldom visiting flowers but frequently resting, with closed wings, usually on a leaf. The brown upper wings are rarely seen as they are only visible when the butterfly is in flight, when the wings move too rapidly to discern any detail.

If you see one or more small butterflies fluttering above the vegetation, stop and look closely in the area where they land: even then, finding them can be a challenge.

The Small Pearl-bordered Fritillary (*Boloria selene*) is a scarce butterfly with just a handful of sites in the Yorkshire Dales and North Pennines, inhabiting wet flushes where their larval food plant, the marsh violet (*Viola palustris*) grows. In the north they appear on the wing in late May, flying for about a month. They are fast fliers but will rest on bracken or heather plants with wings open or closed. The small pearl-bordered fritillary is often mistaken for a wall-brown butterfly or emperor moth which have similar colouring on their upper wings, but the lower wings are much brighter and it is the only actual fritillary to fly in these hills.

The **Green-veined White** (*Pieris napi*) is a common species throughout the British Isles and the most likely of the white butterfly family to be seen on the moors (see image on page 60). It tends to live in groups or colonies,

but there are few larval food plants on the moors which, combined with the poor weather, makes it difficult for the butterfly to become established. It needs wild relatives of the cabbage family (crucifers) on which to lay its eggs, particularly the Cuckoo Flower (or Ladies' Smock) which grows in damp areas. The green-veined white is easy to spot as it is conspicuously white, but when it rests, the grey-green patterning can be seen on the hind-wing veins.

Small pearl-bordered fritillary

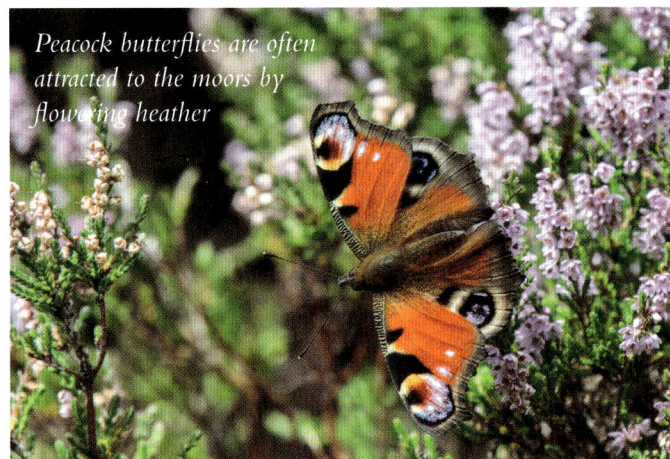
Peacock butterflies are often attracted to the moors by flowering heather

Green hairstreak butterfly on a sprig of crowberry

Glaucous shears moth

MOTHS

Several of the day-flying moths can be seen over the moors, the most abundant of which is the **Common Heath**. This is a small, delicate brown moth with dappled wings that could be found almost anywhere on the moors, usually in May and June where their caterpillars feed on heather (Calluna and Erica).

The **Emperor Moth** (*Saturnia pavonia*) is a large and beautiful insect with distinctive eye spots on its wings. Both sexes are on the wing in April and May but you are only likely to see the orange-winged males in flight during the day, as they search for the torpid, grey females, who only fly at night. Virgin females release a pheromone which can attract males from far and wide. The males are not easy to photograph because they tend not to settle much during daylight hours, and can easily be mistaken for butterflies. Females are conspicuous among the vegetation and are more sedentary in the daytime.

Emperor moth caterpillar

The **Northern Eggar Moth** *(Lasiocampa quercus)* is the northern form of the more widespread oak eggar, although they are usually considered to be the same species. It can be seen flying erratically over the moors during mid to late summer, especially on warm afternoons. The day-flying male is larger and darker brown than the female which takes to the wing from early dusk.

The name 'eggar' is derived from the egg-shaped cocoon, which is produced by the huge hairy caterpillars. These are a common sight on the moors during June and July, where their main food plants are bilberry and heather. Eggar moth caterpillars are a favourite food of cuckoos.

The **Glaucous Shears Moth** *(Papestra biren)* is a moorland specialist, distributed quite sparsely across the north and west of Britain. Their speckled grey colouration is camouflage as they often rest on tree bark or wooden posts. Their caterpillars feed mainly on heather on the moors.

The **Fox Moth** *(Macrothylacia rubi)* is another large, brown moth, which has similar habits to the northern eggar but with plainer wing colouring. The males fly close to the ground searching for females, but again, are fast so difficult to examine closely or photograph.

Northern eggar moth

Fox moth

The **Smoky Wave Moth** (*Scopula ternata*) is very common on the Peak District moors, flying during the daytime where its caterpillars feed on both heather and bilberry. 'Scopula' means little broom, because some members of the genus have a small brush–like appendage on the hind legs.

Another moorland moth that can be seen by day during the summer months, most usually from July onwards, is the **True Lover's Knot** (*Lycophotia porphyrea*), which is a moorland specialist. Its caterpillars feed on heather plants. It is about an inch (25mm) long with chestnut, black and white markings. The **Antler Moth** (*Cerapteryx graminis*) is also common on heaths and downs over much of the British Isles. On higher ground they can be numerous and are capable of destroying extensive areas of grass.

Ear Moths (*Amphipoea sp.*) are widely distributed in damp places where their caterpillars feed low down on the stems and roots of grasses. There are a number of species which can only be told apart through dissection.

Smoky wave moth

BUMBLEBEES

Many of the common bumblebees which frequent field borders and gardens at lower altitudes are tempted to the moors by the heather flowers where they carry out their essential function of pollination.

However, there is a rare upland specialist, which is the **Bilberry Bumblebee** (*Bombus monticola*), named after its liking for bilberry flowers in the early spring. This smallish bumblebee has a hairy, orange abdomen and black thorax. Unlike the more common species, it feeds on bell heather and cross-leaved heather but does not feed on common heather. This seems somewhat bizarre when calluna abounds on many moors.

Buff-tailed Bumblebees (*Bombus terrestris*) are misleadingly named as only the queens have a buff tail: their workers and drones have off-white tails. They are one of the most common bumblebees in Britain and are frequently seen on the moors.

White-tailed Bumblebee (*Bombus lucorum*) is another common lowland species that can be found on the moors. The queens have white tails but the other castes can be similar to buff-tails, though the yellow is a paler lemon colour compared with the orange-yellow of buff-tails.

Red-tailed Bumblebee (*Bombus lapidarius*) is usually all black with an orange tail. But males can have two yellow stripes on the thorax making them very similar to the rare bilberry bumblebee, whose abdomen is orange rather than just the tail.

These are all common widespread bumblebees that are tempted onto the moors by any suitable nectar sources, favouring the bilberry in the spring and all three heather species in the summer.

Bilberry bumblebee

BEETLES

A lot of beetle species occur in the Pennines but are hidden away in fallen trees, leaf litter, hedgerows and so on. The few species covered here all live on the surface as adults and are large enough to be easily seen.

Sexton beetle

This is a family of several species all of which have distinctive orange patches on the elytra. They fly for miles to reach anything dead, and when they arrive they will attempt to bury the corpse. In the photograph, a **Common Sexton Beetle** *(Nicrophorus vespilloides)* has found a dead field vole, accompanied by a large fly. Although a small mammal, the vole seems to present something of a challenge to the beetle if it is to be buried.

The beetle lays its eggs in the buried material which then provides food for its hatching larvae. 'Sexton' is a formal name for a church officer whose duty includes the digging of graves.

Beetles play a major role in clearing the countryside of organic remains and thereby fertilising the soil. One example of this is the **Dor Beetle** *(Geotrupes stercorarius)*. It is quite large (c2.5cm) with iridescent black armour and strong spiky legs for tunnelling. Both males and females dig tunnels with lots of side chambers underneath cow pats in which they store some cow dung where the female lays an egg. Dor beetles can be found anywhere that cows have not been dosed with anti-worming drugs. The name Dor is an old English word for bumblebee.

Oil beetles

Species of oil beetle in the Pennines include the **Violet Oil Beetle** *(Meloe violaceus)* and the Black Oil Beetle *(M. proscarabeus)*. They can be found on the moors where the adult beetles feed on vegetation and lay eggs in the soil. When the eggs hatch into larvae, they climb onto flower heads where they wait for visiting solitary bees. The larva

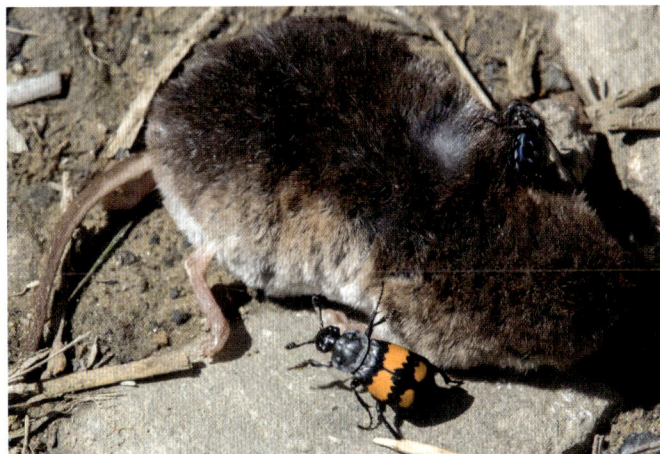

Sexton beetle

Violet oil beetle

Dor beetle

clamps onto the bee and is transported back to the bee's nest where it feeds on the bee's eggs and any pollen or nectar the bee has collected. It pupates in the bee's nest and emerges in the spring to fly off and find a mate. They have under-developed wing cases and swollen abdomens, and they are called oil beetles because they exude a noxious oil when handled.

FLIES

Many flies inhabit the Pennine moors and they are probably the most important airborne food source for insectivorous birds. Craneflies have already been discussed in Chapter 1, but there are also many gnats, midges, hover flies and true flies involved in decomposition and parasitism, each with its niche in the ecosystem. Although the *Diptera* species are numerous and important, they are incredibly diverse, with around 600 species of *Tipulid* in Britain alone, so they are not described further here.

Curlew

BIRDS OF THE UPLAND HEATHS

Views over the Pennine moors are usually across an expanse of low heather, bilberry and moor grass with no cover apart from the odd copse of birch. The beauty is in the stately rise and fall of the landscape and the cloud patterns in the sky rather than the easy intimacy of a leafy glade or flower meadow. The birds that inhabit the Pennine moors full-time are specialists which do not need trees and who can find cover among the leggy heather and bracken, in which they take refuge at any sign of danger. The melancholy warbling whistle of the curlew is characteristic of heaths and lowland marshes, and they are frequently to be seen in flight, calling as they go. Red grouse can be quite relaxed about human presence and meadow pipits will watch you before flying off a few metres to find a safer perch.

Raptors are likely to be seen in the distance, patrolling the heaths for prey, and it can be well worth taking some time out to sit and watch to see what unfolds.

The best time of year for moorland birds is the spring and early summer, as most birds leave the uplands once their chicks have fledged, leaving only the resident grouse to defend their winter territories.

Red Grouse *(Lagopus lagopus)*. This native game bird inhabits and breeds on the upland moors of Great Britain and Ireland. It has reddish-brown plumage with pale-feathered legs and a plump appearance. Both sexes have red combs over the eyes but on the males these are larger and can be pumped up to be more conspicuous when they are breeding or fighting. Its principle food is heather, although it will eat berries and invertebrates. Their call is a rapidly repeated sound rather like a duck quack cut short.

The grouse pair up during the autumn and are territorial during the winter. Usually eight well-camouflaged yellowish eggs are laid during April and May in shallow scrapes, hatching three weeks later.

The **Curlew** *(Numenius arquata*) nests among long vegetation, but is not particularly a heathland specialist, as it will nest in meadows and pastures too. Outside the breeding season they move off and can be found around Britain's coasts, waterways and moors. In the Pennines, they feed on worms, insects and even some larger prey like young frogs.

They are ground nesting, building quite a large nest by scraping a hollow and lining it with grass and other soft vegetation. About four eggs are laid and, once they hatch, the chicks are looked after by the parents for around six weeks.

The two distinctive features of the curlew are its long curved bill and its plaintive call, so evocative of bleak open spaces.

Golden Plover *(Pluvialis apricaria)* breed on the moors from May to August, taking advantage of the abundance of insect food in summer. As they are resident primarily in the blanket bogs, the species has been covered in Chapter 1.

The **Meadow Pipit** *(Anthus pratensis)* is the most common songbird on the moors during the summer months, flying to lower feeding grounds in the winter. They are most prevalent in mixed habitats where grass, heather and bog are all found and they feed on flies, beetles, moths and spiders. They often have two broods in the season, nesting on the ground under thick vegetation and laying three to five speckled brown eggs.

Their upper plumage is a striped brown, whilst they are almost white with dark streaks below, blending well with their favourite habitat. A small brown bird with white outer tail feathers and calling a repeated seep, seep, seep as it flies between perches is the view that most Pennine visitors will have. In early spring they are more demonstrative, performing elaborate parachuting flights as they sing.

Meadow pipit

Meadow Pipit nests are taken over by cuckoos in the Pennines, which is hard on them as the adult pipit is much, much smaller than the cuckoo chick by the time it fledges.

Cuckoos *(Cuculus canorus)* are present from April for only a few months and return to Africa before their young have fledged from pipit nests. The cuckoo is strong in English tradition as a harbinger of spring and their arrival is still celebrated annually at the Marsden Cuckoo

A cuckoo in flight over heather

Festival in West Yorkshire. Sadly, cuckoo numbers have declined so severely that their distinctive call is heard far less often than it was.

Like the cuckoo, **Whinchats** *(Saxicola rubetra)* are summer migrant visitors, arriving from sub-Saharan Africa in April to nest on bracken litter in small patches of fern among a mosaic of upland vegetation. They tend to perch on the highest vantage point available and can be recognised by the light-coloured stripe above the eye. Their song is a repetitive scolding 'hueet tic-tic, tic-tic'. Their main diet is insects.

Whinchats are rapidly declining throughout their range, and in the UK are not helped by the practice of burning the heath, as it removes bracken litter and destroys their nesting habitat.

Ring ouzel

Ring Ouzels *(Turdus torquatus)* are a scarce upland cousins of the blackbird, but unlike blackbirds they are summer visitors from their wintering grounds in the Atlas

Whinchat on bracken

Twite on bracken

Mountains of North Africa. They are distinguished by a pale crescent on the breast, known as a gorget, which is also the name for the breast plate in a suit of armour. The males are more striking as they have blacker plumage than the females and their gorget is usually pure white rather than stained. They prefer to nest in rocky gullies, usually among a clump of heather, raising two or three broods each season. The male takes care of the fledgling youngsters while the female incubates the next batch of eggs.

Ring ouzels feed in grassy areas, usually where there are also patches of heather and bracken. Until the bilberries are ripe, they feed on worms in damp weather and then switch to caterpillars if it is dry. Then when the berries appear, they gorge themselves to fuel their migration to Africa.

Twite *(Carduelis flavirostris).* In a restricted area between Halifax and Rochdale in the south Pennines a small population of 100 pairs of twite survive. They nest on upland heath, usually in bracken litter but do most of their feeding in nearby hay meadows. It is a finch, closely related to the linnet. Its upper plumage is brown with dark streaks and lighter underneath and almost the only truly distinguishing diagnostic feature is a pink rump in the males.

Twite can be seen in the Pennine uplands from late March to September after which the Pennine birds move to the east coast of England for the winter.

They are unusual in that they feed their young entirely on seeds, whereas most seed-eating British songbirds switch to an insect diet to feed their chicks, and this is a likely cause of their decline as a species. Their seed diet is sourced from hay meadows where a variety of flowers and grasses grow, but we have lost 97% of these hay meadows, mainly to silage production. Even the few remaining hay meadows tend to be cut too early for the mature seeds that the twite relies upon, to develop. In an attempt to reverse this, organisations like the RSPB have been working with farmers in the area to revert some land to late-cut hay meadow, which would benefit not only the twite, but many other birds and insects.

The **Dotterel** *(Charadrius morinellus)* is a rare, migratory member of the plover family which arrives in the UK in April and May, then spends the summer in the highest parts of England and Scotland. Unusually, the female has brighter plumage than the male, who also incubates the eggs and rears the chicks.

Dotterel

A recently fledged juvenile merlin, the smallest raptor in Britain

BIRDS OF PREY

Several of Britain's raptors frequent the Pennine uplands, as there is food and space for them there, although some are becoming very rare and not at all easy to find. The kestrel is the most common and the most easily seen, as it hovers searching for prey on the ground below: it is the only bird of prey in Britain that does this habitually, though buzzards hover occasionally. Rocky outcrops, and also telegraph wires, provide perches from which they can monitor the landscape and readily take flight.

The **Merlin** *(Falco columbarius)* is another falcon and the smallest British bird of prey. They nest at low density throughout the Pennines and could be regarded as the specialist raptor of the Pennine moors. They leave the uplands in the autumn for fens and estuaries, returning in March and April to nest in very deep heather, or occasionally in old crows' nests in trees.

The merlin is inconspicuous and difficult to see as it flies fast and low over moorland and never hovers. Their favourite prey are meadow pipits which they chase through the air if necessary, 'locking-on' to their quarry and following every twist and turn in the air. They also eat other small birds and lots of large moths, such as emperor, northern eggar and fox moths.

Kestrel *(Falco tinnunculus)*. When these small falcons are resident in the Pennines, they nest on rocky cliffs and feed mainly on field voles but also birds and insects. They can be easily identified by their frequent habit of hovering and their shape and colouring is quite distinctive, being terracotta above and pale beneath, while the male has a black-tipped blue tail.

A kestrel hovering

Kestrels nest in the spring, laying up to four eggs on separate days, out of which one to three chicks will normally fledge depending on the availability of food and the severity of the weather.

Peregrine *(Falco peregrinus)* is not an upland specialist, being found throughout the United Kingdom, but they love a high perch and nest on inaccessible cliffs, so they do favour the rocky ledges on Pennine crags. This large and powerful falcon has great wings with pointed ends. Like the merlin, it is a swift flier and can chase its prey, but more characteristically it stoops on prey from a great height. In its descent it is reputed to be the fastest creature on the planet, achieving speeds up to 200mph.

Their colouring is steely blue on its upper body and wings, with a striking black and white head pattern, while its breast is much paler and finely barred.

Peregrines have also been persecuted, reaching a low point in the 1960s due to human persecution and the impact of pesticides which resulted in fragile egg shells which cracked when the bird incubated them. Numbers have been recovering nationally, largely owing to its colonisation of urban areas.

Peregrine in flight

Short-eared owl

The typical food of the **Hen Harrier** (*Circus cyaneus*) are meadow pipits and voles, but this has not stopped it being regarded as a predatory nuisance. It has been saddled with its unfortunate name and reputation because in times past, when domestic fowl were allowed to roam freely, some would have been taken by it as easy prey. This is a frequent phenomenon around the world, as humans encroach upon a wild animal's territory, causing a change in its behaviour which results in the wild resident being demonised as dangerous or vermin. In such cases, the human commercial value almost always trumps the fact that the animal was there long before humans arrived.

The hen harrier remains the most intensively persecuted of the UK's birds of prey (although it has survived, unlike the red kite which was persecuted to

Short-eared Owls (*Asio flammeus*) – see title page – are the most frequently encountered day-flying owl in the Pennines and are regarded as full-time residents, although some descend to the lowlands for winter. They feed largely on short-tailed voles whose numbers oscillate between boom and bust in successive years, so the number of owls varies accordingly. They can be seen flying throughout the day, but are most active at dusk and dawn.

They are ground-nesting, laying up to thirteen eggs when voles are abundant. Incubation starts when the first egg is laid and a further egg follows on each subsequent day so that they hatch at intervals and the chicks in the nest vary in size. The largest chick, which will be the earliest laid, gets the first choice of food and the rest have to take their turn, meaning that the later chicks in a large brood have a hard time making it to fledging unless voles are abundant. This is a strategy to ensure that the maximum number of chicks survive whatever the abundance of food.

Female hen harrier

extinction in almost all of the UK until reintroduced at the end of the twentieth century). On the Pennine moors, it does predate on grouse chicks as well as voles, which makes it the gamekeeper's enemy. On grouse moors here and elsewhere, the species is teetering on the verge of extinction. As the moors are its natural habitat, birds move in from non-shooting areas and, when that occurs, nests have to be kept under 24 hour guard. Sadly, even this does not ensure success as males often fail to return when they go hunting on the grouse moors.

Males are a pale grey colour with black wing tips while females and immature birds are brown with a white rump and are known collectively as ringtails. They have a gliding flight, travelling low over the heather in search of food with wings held in a shallow 'V'.

A female Hen harrier soars over Castle Hill in Huddersfield

REPTILES AND AMPHIBIANS IN UPLAND HEATHS

The Pennine weather is seldom on the side of cold-blooded reptiles and amphibians, especially at higher altitudes, so this is on the northern edge of their range. However **Adders** *(Vipera berus)*, and **Common Lizards** *(Zootoca vivipara)* do occur on many of the heaths and moors where they hibernate through the winter, becoming active in the warmer weather. Adders feed largely on common lizards on the moors, but will go for frogs, voles, small birds and bird eggs.

Common lizards are also known as viviparous lizards because they give birth to live young. They can often be found on sunny mornings, warming themselves on a dry-stone wall, ready to scurry away between the cracks in the stones at any sign of danger.

Above: Common lizard
Right: Adder

MAMMALS IN UPLAND HEATHS

The **Field Vole** *(Microtus agrestis)* has tiny ears and eyes, a blunt snout, a short tail and dull shaggy brown fur that is rather sparse and doesn't look very warm. They are largely herbivorous, eating grasses and herbs, but can also consume insects. Although this little brown rodent cannot be regarded as an upland heath specialist, being common throughout the United Kingdom, it is extremely important as a source of food, particularly for the upland birds. Luckily, they breed prolifically in winter as well as summer months, the females producing up to seven litters of up to six young each year. This rapid reproduction is possible because the young are weaned within a fortnight.

A field vole

They run very fast through passages in grassland known as vole runs, marking their territory with urine. Sadly for them, urine glows under UV light, and birds of prey have eyes with UV-sensitive cells so they can readily observe a vole run and see where a vole has just urinated. Hovering kestrels will often have been attracted by fluorescing urine.

If one proceeds quietly, **Mountain Hares** *(Lepus timidus)* can often be seen on the Pennine moors, even at close quarters. They were introduced to the Peak District in the nineteenth century to add variety at shoots. Ironically they are now persecuted by shooting interests because they can carry blood-sucking ticks which transmit a disease called louping-ill to grouse which inhabit the same area.

They are slightly smaller than the brown hare and, although they are a similar colour to the brown hare in the warmer months, their fur turns white in the winter. Mountain hares feed mostly on grass, but if that is scarce they will tackle woody shrubs.

Of course many of the mammals you will encounter on the Pennine uplands are species which thrive anywhere in the UK where they have sufficient wild land to roam undisturbed by man. While in this book we have tried to focus on the specialist species that a walker has a good

A mountain hare in its white winter coat bounding over moors

chance of seeing, it would be remiss not to include on this spread a few of Britain's most iconic mammals that live in the Pennines.

Stoat

Brown hare

Roe deer

PLACES TO FIND UPLAND HEATH HABITATS

Great tracts of upland heath are to be found over the length of the Pennine hills below the highest tops and more where the land is sloping so water can run off. Heath, bog and grassland often run into each other and land use strongly affects the appearance and content.

Upland heath SSSIs

Name	Location	Size	Grid Ref.
MSH–2 Mallerstang Common	North Pennines	45000	NY 804050
MSH–3 Pickersett and Hood Rigg	North Pennines	45000	SD 855964
Moor House – Upper Teesdale	Upper Teesdale	38803	NY799358
South Pennine Moors	Ilkley to Peaks	20938	SD 920300
West Nidderdale, Barden and Blubberhouses	Between Wharfedale and Nidderdale	13419	SE 080705
East Nidderdale Moors	Nidderdale	10777	SE 112854
Lovely Seat – Stainton Moor	Stainton Moor	10128	SD 863933
Arkengarthdale, Gunnerside & Reeth Moors	Arkengarthdale	7634	NY 935070

The main limestone areas in the Pennines (marked in purple)

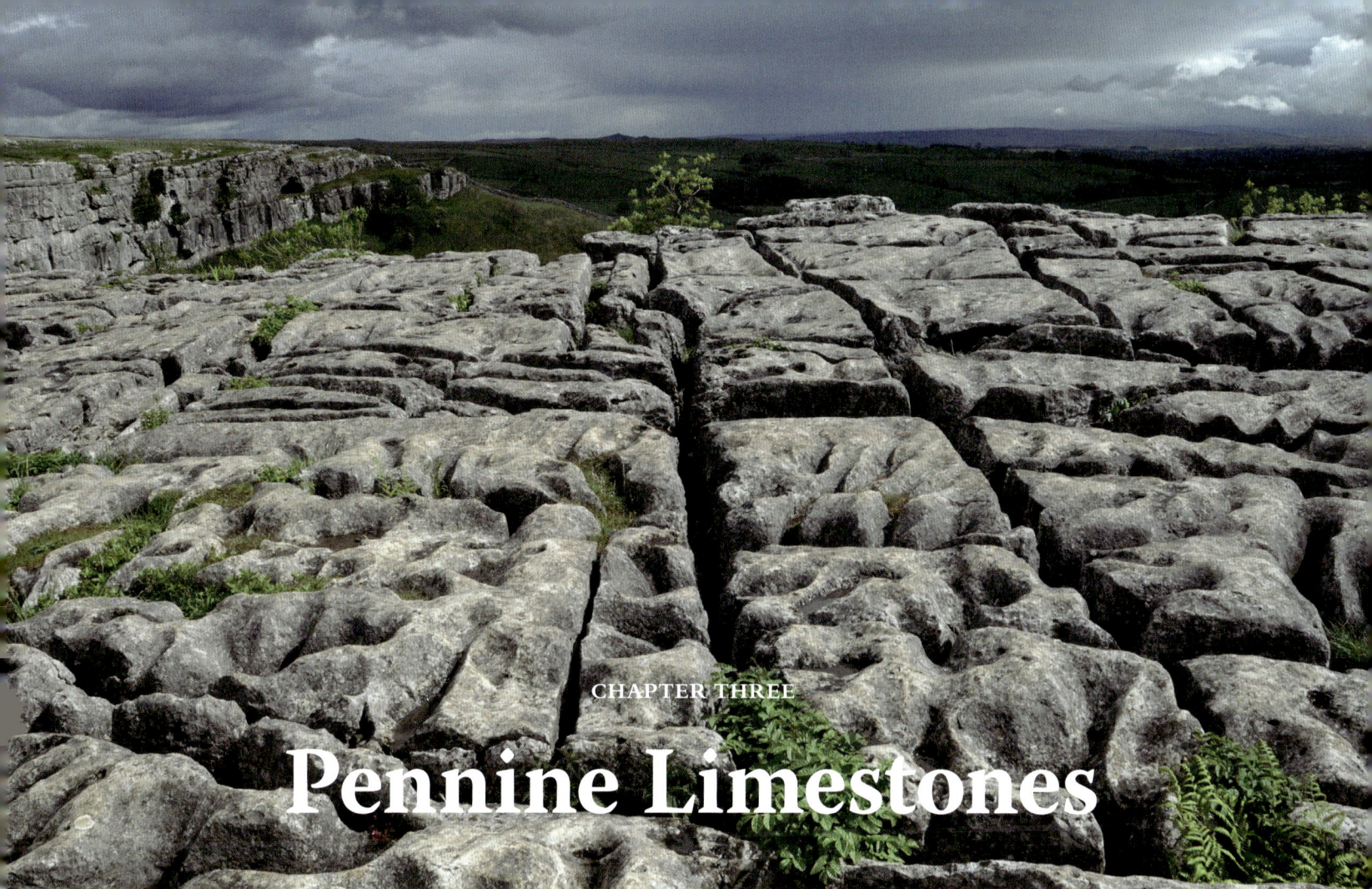

CHAPTER THREE

Pennine Limestones

When the moors give way to limestone, everything in the landscape changes, which is one of the great charms of the Pennine Hills. Both blanket bog and upland heath have a similar 'look and feel', whether on the moors outside Chesterfield in the south or in the rural idyll of Arkengarthdale Moor in the north: the hills are rounded and the huge stretches of moor are covered in heather, rough grasses and bilberry.

The three main areas in which limestone is exposed in the Pennines are the Derbyshire Peak District, the Yorkshire Dales and Upper Teesdale, each containing a variety of landscapes and possessing a truly unique character. Moving from acid moor or bog to limestone, the dominant vegetation changes to grassland, most of which is grazed, and woods. The huge heaths, blanket bogs and pools are replaced by a dramatic landscape of crags, caves and green grass. This contrast has resulted in the Peak District being divided into the 'Dark Peak', where moors and millstone grit prevail, and the 'White Peak' where limestone is the bedrock and deep dales characterised by

Above: a hay meadow in the Peak District

grey cliffs and crags cut across the rolling green pastures patterned with drystone walls.

The reason for all this is that limestone is made up largely of calcium carbonate which gradually dissolves as water flows over it, a chemical reaction turning it to calcium hydroxide which makes the water slightly alkaline. Rain landing on a limestone surface finds any cracks and, over millennia, weathers the rock, widening the cracks such that they can eventually grow into limestone pavement or potholes and caverns. As it erodes the surface, water carves the cliffs, crags and deep dales which bestow such variety and beauty on the landscape.

Surface water tends to sink down the many faults in the limestone, carrying any loose silt with it, so the soil is shallow and the moisture it contains will be slightly alkaline, contrasting sharply with the water of the bogs and moors, which is acidic. Therefore, plants that grow on limestone are lime-loving, or calcicole, as opposed to lime-hating, or calcifuge, which is what the Pennine heathers are. So it is that a lot of the surface is covered in palatable grasses and, if the land is not fertilised or over-grazed, these will be mixed with a rich variety of herbs and orchids which attract insects.

Much of the land that is now agricultural was once tree-covered, but most of the natural (not plantation) woodlands that remain are situated where the land is too steep to farm easily. This is particularly the case along the river valleys, or dales where the dominant tree species is ash, usually along with hazel and hawthorn and, in the oldest woods, with wych elm.

As a result of urban development and the intensification of farming, unploughed limestone grasslands such as those found in the Pennines have become rare habitats, which is sad as they are often very rich in species and simply gorgeous when the flowers are in bloom. The disappearance of flower meadows and unimproved pasture accelerated in the twentieth century with agricultural grants and more intense farming practices: in particular, the change from hay to silage for winter livestock feed. If they weren't mown or grazed, these grasslands would revert to scrub and forest, as they were before people arrived but, as in the upland heaths, the intensity of use and style of management will dictate the quality of the ecosystem and the quantity of species found.

An unimproved pasture in a Peak District dale can contain dozens of species of grasses, sedges, herbs, mosses and lichens, the precise make-up of the plant community depending on the soil depth, moisture levels and acidity (pH). Occasionally a concurrence of both chalky and acid or neutral soil within the same area can exist, enabling even greater diversity. Between the extremes of traditional hay meadows and silage fields, a piece of land can be in a myriad of possible states, some of which are good for both grazing and diversity, and others less so, such as when creeping buttercups or thistles take over. Finding a good equilibrium in the poor, thin soils of the upper Dales can be very challenging.

There are plenty of rivers in the limestone uplands, but only one natural lake of any size, which is Malham Tarn in the Yorkshire Dales. The reason that water has been able to collect here is that there is a dip in the land where the underlying rock is Silurian silt-stone, an ancient sedimentary rock which, like millstone grit, is impervious to water. This also explains the sizeable raised peat marsh on the west bank of the Tarn.

Farmland in the White Peak District in Derbyshire, above Millers Dale

THE PEAK DISTRICT

At the southern end of the Pennines, the hills that rise from the Derbyshire and Staffordshire plains are the limestone dales of the Peak District, known as the White Peak. Moors rise to the east and west of the limestone as the cap of millstone grit persists in these areas, but where this ends and limestone takes over, the change can be quite abrupt. For instance, to the east of Stoney Middleton the land climbs steeply to the millstone grit cliffs of Froggatt Edge, and behind that is an expanse of acid moorland covered in heather and moor-grass. Immediately to the west lie Middleton Dale, Litton Dale and Cressbrook Dale, where a patchwork of grey drystone walled and green pastures plunges down over limestone crags to limestone grasslands and woods below. Between these dales, the landscape is gently rolling grassy fields containing many sheep, and dotted with farms and settlements. It is a highly managed rural landscape in which the uniform green is maintained by fertilisers and grazing. Nature reasserts herself in the deep water-cut valleys where limestone cliffs, crags and pinnacles shoot up from tumbling rivers such as the Dove, the Wye, and the Manifold. The overall effect of the landscape is varied and pretty, rather than bleak and imposing as on the moors, and natural habitats are smaller in extent and more varied.

The Peak District is one of the more populated areas in the Pennines, with many textile and mining industry settlements. The area was the richest in Britain for copper

Monsal Dale, carved out by the river Wye and photographed from Monsal Dale Head

and lead which were mined from the Bronze Age until the late nineteenth century. Today, around the remaining ruins and spoil heaps, some of the land has high concentrations of mineral residues, particularly lead, which changes and limits the range of plants species that can grow. This sort of habitat and the specialist plants that thrive there, are covered in greater detail later in the book.

In addition to grassland and limestone crags, there is quite a lot of woodland in the Peak District, especially in the dales and along rivers. Oddly, there are also a few areas of limestone heath where acid-loving plants are able to grow: this is because the limestone bedrock has become overlaid with deep wind-blown soil (known as 'loess') or else it has a layer of glacial moraine. In either case, the wind-blown deposits 'insulate' the surface soil from the limestone beneath, enabling the accumulation of water which remains chemically unaffected by the calcium

Left: Looking west along the Hope Valley in the Peak District from the Millstone Grit crags of Stanage Edge. The sandstone continues to the moorlands in the middle of this picture, which is the start of the 'Dark Peak'. The limestone White Peak starts on the south side of the green valley on the left.

below. Longstone Moor in Derbyshire is an example, where the underlying rock is limestone, but the dominant vegetation is common heath and bilberry, neither of which is normally seen on the limestone grasslands.

The northern limit of the White Peak is at Castleton and the spectacular limestone gorge of Winnats Pass, beyond which the gritstone mass of Mam Tor rises, marking the beginning of the Dark Peak. From the north side of the Hope Valley, which runs between Castleton and Hathersage, the landscape is moorland for 70 miles until limestone breaks the surface once more north of Skipton. This is the start of the Yorkshire Dales where the glacially-formed landscape is on a much grander scale than in the Derbyshire Dales.

THE YORKSHIRE DALES

Overall, the land in the Dales is higher than in the Peaks and has been more obviously formed by Ice Age glaciers which scraped out U-shaped valleys as they flowed, exposing long scars of bare rock. This is particularly apparent on the sides of the 'Three Peaks' of Great Whernside, Ingleborough and Pen-y-Ghent which tower up from the rivers and grasslands. There are extensive areas where topsoil never forms as it is washed away down the cracks in the limestone bedrock, leaving bare 'karst'. This is where the naked limestone has weathered to form pavements, gullies, towers and isolated boulders, known as 'erratics'.

Soil has accumulated where the land is reasonably level and the underlying limestone has not been fractured and cracked. This is almost all grassy and used to raise sheep and cattle in fields separated by drystone walls. The soil is deepest in the river valleys and tends to get thinner as the land climbs, so farming becomes increasingly tenuous as the limestone is seen more at the surface. At about 380 metres altitude, the karst landscape often takes over, most spectacularly between Horton-in-Ribbleside and Ingleton where huge areas of limestone pavement are exposed. In such places, the surface is bare rock and the only plants that may be seen breaking the surface are isolated yew or hawthorn trees, rooted in the soil in the gaps in the pavement, known as 'grykes'. These trees are

Limestone pavement, a karst landscape in the Yorkshire Dales with Ingleborough in the background

Swinner Gill in Swaledale in the Yorkshire Dales, looking into a limestone ravine with the moors behind which are spread across sandstone that is sitting on the limestone

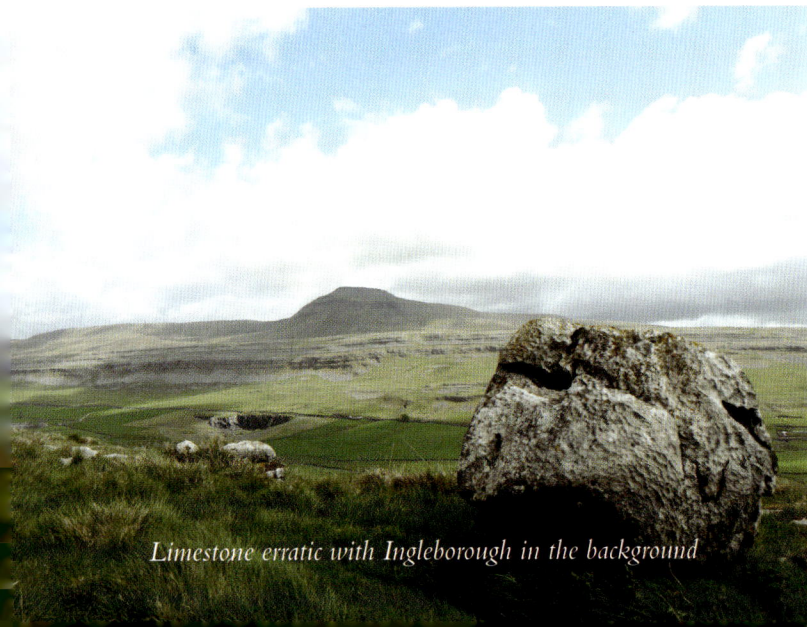

Limestone erratic with Ingleborough in the background

usually gnarled and bent by the harsh, windy conditions. However, it is a different story within the grykes, which are sheltered and which benefit from any silt washed off the surface and wind-blown particles. In these deep crevices, plants of many types take root, particularly ferns, along with mosses and liverworts, so that each gryke will have its own little community. Above about 450 metres, the limestone usually gives way to a cap of sandstone and millstone grit, and the habitat reverts to acid moorland.

There are a number of coniferous plantations in the Yorkshire Dales, mostly on steep hillsides which were planted in the twentieth century, but very few native broad-leaved woods remain. Those that are still standing are mostly along the course of waterways, such as in Wharfedale, which contains a cluster of woodland SSSIs including Bastow Wood near Grassington. The predominant tree species is ash, with an understorey of hazel and wych elm. The ground flora is dominated by dog's mercury, wild garlic and grasses interspersed with herbs such as rockrose, fairy flax and woodland orchids.

In a few locations, ancient oak-birch woodland grows where slate is the base rock. The soil tends to be acid so the ground flora is dominated by great wood-rush and bilberry and there is an abundance of mosses and liverworts. There are also a good number of sycamore trees and copses spread about the dales, either planted or self-seeded.

Rivers descend steep slopes and waterfalls are quite common, particularly where a ledge of harder rock overlays soluble limestone. The water is unpolluted, so brown trout occur and, in some rivers, salmon can be seen leaping up the cascades in September, heading for spawning grounds. This is also where dippers are commonly seen on the rocks along fast-flowing streams.

The Yorkshire Dales limestone peters out to the north of Swaledale and acid moorland rises to Rogan's Seat at 672 metres and continues to the National Park boundary at Britain's highest pub, the Tan Hill Inn.

UPPER TEESDALE

Following the Pennine Way from Tan Hill to the north of the Yorkshire Dales National Park, the land dips into the Greta Valley, and the Roman road that is now the A67 crosses the Pennine moors between Barnard Castle and Appleby-in-Westmoreland. Continuing north for about 10 miles over the treeless Lune Forest, the Pennine Way skirts the Moorhouse Upper Tees National Nature Reserve on the south side of Teesdale and the river Tees.

The geology of Upper Teesdale is quite complex, with a mosaic of limestone, sugar limestone, sedimentary rocks and quartz dolerite creating a variety of habitats on the surface including hay meadows, juniper woods, limestone grasslands and blanket bogs.

The sugar limestone areas, mainly to the south and west of Middleton-in-Teesdale, contain a number of post-

Low Force waterfall in Teesdale which cascades from the hard rock of Whin Sill

Winnats Pass at the top of the Hope Valley in Derbyshire. The steep sides of this water-cut pass are covered in grassy pastures which are grazed by sheep but are otherwise unimproved. They are rich in lime-loving grasses, sedges and herbs. Apart from the sheep, snails which share the grazing rights are also to be found clinging to the crags (see facing page).

glacial arctic and alpine plants which survive here since the last Ice Age, known as The Teesdale Assemblage. Sugar limestone occurs where limestone has been modified by heat and pressure that it was subjected to 295 million years ago, when a mass of magma, known to geologists as Whin Sill, pushed into it. Sugar limestone has a more blotched appearance than the carboniferous limestone and tends to crumble into a sugary grit.

There are grasslands and flushes in Teesdale which are among the most botanically rich in upland Britain, containing an unparalleled range of rare plants, some of which occur nowhere else in Britain. Because of the complex geology in the area and the nature of the limestone, Upper Teesdale does not have the appearance of a typical limestone landscape, although there are caves and some spectacular waterfalls. The area, especially where the rare flowers flourish, is quite remote, with a low human population and only small settlements which put less pressure on the landscape than the more populated south.

WILDLIFE IN THE LIMESTONE UPLANDS

Where limestone is the bedrock, it provides a harsh environment for plants to grow in, as its soils retain neither water nor nutrients very well and the limey soils make it more difficult for plants to absorb certain minerals, such as iron. However, many rare and lovely wild flowers thrive in these conditions, so it is plants that are the main focus of this chapter.

Limestone habitats tend to contain fewer of the most common plants that thrive in fertilised conditions, such as docks, nettles, thistles and coarse grasses. However, the great majority of walled pastures in the Peaks and the Dales have been fertilised by sheep droppings, manure or chemical fertilisers and some have been sown with rye grass for yield efficiency. In addition, sheep nibble the verdure very low, which means that many plants cannot get a foothold: in such cases, a field of grass may contain very few species.

On the lower slopes of the limestone dales in the springtime, you will see many fields and verges covered in buttercups, clover and ox-eye daisies, which are easy on the eye, but not truly wild-flower meadows, which are far more diverse.

Grove Snails (*Cepaea nemoralis*) *are common on the grassy slopes of the dales: these were in the outcrop on the left of the picture on the facing page, in a limestone crevice. They come out to feed on grass*

Traditional flower meadows are not fertilised and mowing takes place once the flowers have dropped their seeds so that more specialised and unusual plants can thrive. There are very few such unimproved flower meadows surviving across England, and the Yorkshire Dales possess the greatest number of any region, most of which are protected as SSSIs. Diverse flora including rare species can also be found in woods, rocky places and wet flushes: usually where sheep can't or won't go.

In 2018, the National Trust bought nearly 200 hectares of grassland in the White Peak District in two locations which are currently a mixture of pasture, silage, rough grassland and meadow. The overarching objective is to contribute to restoring species-rich grassland and biodiversity in the area. This is a welcome initiative as it changes the purpose of land management from providing an income to developing a rich ecosystem of a type that was once common in the area but is now extremely rare.

Close examination of a natural limestone turf will reveal plants with differing habits and leaf shapes clustered together, which only an expert botanist can distinguish by eye. Among the more common plants that can be found are cowslip, wild thyme, rock-rose and bird's-foot trefoil, whilst rarer or more specialised flowers might include globeflower and a number of orchid species.

As these plants flower at different times between March and October, a diverse meadow can be colourful for many months and provides food and a breeding ground for a great variety of insects and other invertebrates. The seeds provide sustenance for voles and birds such as the linnet while the insects are a critical food source for golden plovers and many other species.

Liverworts and mosses inside a gryke in the Dales

Within these three limestone areas of the Pennines are found rocky crags, limestone pavements, grasslands, pastures and meadows, including a large proportion of our remaining unimproved flower meadow, woods, waterways and acid bog and heath. We will now explore the species that are most typical of limestone uplands, or which are an important component of these habitats; however, those which are not limestone specialists are covered in the following chapter on grasslands.

The limestone crags and pavements are a very different habitat from the grasslands, and much harsher, as soil is often absent and where it is found, it can be thin and nutrient-deficient. Plants do grow where soil builds up on cliff ledges and in the crevices which criss-cross limestone pavements (known as grykes), and at the entrances to caves. Plants here include Jacob's ladder, ferns such as the hard shield fern, liverworts and mosses and a few hardy trees including ash and hawthorn. The large liverwort (above) was photographed in a gryke on the flanks of Great Whernside.

Vibrant habitats are found where streams and small rivers tumbling steeply down from the heights have carved steep valleys and waterfalls. The valley sides are often wooded and the ground can be carpeted with bluebells and wild garlic (ramsons) during the spring and a variety of ferns during summer months. Such woods are home to many common birds such as blue tits and chaffinches whilst dippers are encountered on rocks in the middle of the stream and grey or pied wagtails roam the vegetation that lines it.

Wharfedale slope near Grassington with drystone walls and field barns. Hawthorn trees are in blossom

Baneberry flowering in a limestone gryke

ROCKY HABITATS

The Yorkshire Dales are famed for their limestone pavements which are high, very exposed and lack any surface soil. However, within the gaps and cracks in the pavements, plants are sheltered from the wind and soil remains damp, providing good conditions for quite a variety of them. Occasionally a hawthorn, juniper or ash tree manages to get established, rooted in a soil-rich gryke, and these stand out prominently as they are usually very isolated (see page 86). In most cases, tree species have great difficulty in reaching up beyond the top of the gryke, so they grow very slowly, rather in the manner of Japanese bonsai. A number of specialist herbs are found in limestone crevices and on ledges, but you may also come across such plants as mountain mellick grass, or herbs such as dog's mercury, angular solomon's seal and downy currant, although they are not easy to spot. Some quite surprising colonists can occasionally be found which don't seem to belong there, but whose seeds may have been dropped by a bird and are able to take advantage of the sheltered conditions.

FERNS OF THE LIMESTONE UPLANDS

Ferns, mosses and liverworts growing in grykes and crevices can become larger and more luxuriant than specimens growing on the surface as disturbance is minimal. Some of the ferns that are typical of this limestone habitat are described overleaf.

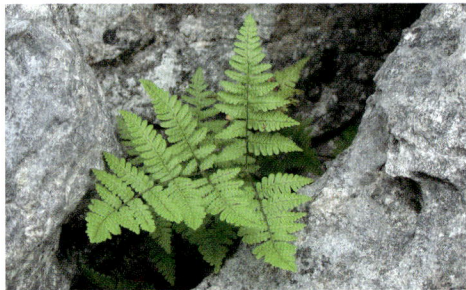

*The limestone fern
(Gymnocarpium robertianum)*

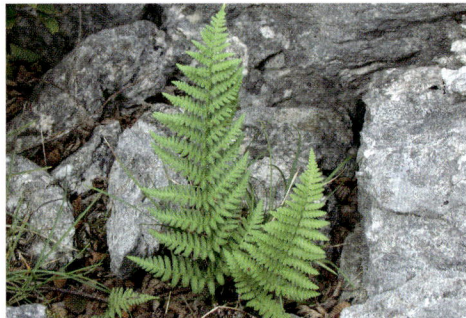

*Rigid buckler fern
(Dryopteris submontana)*

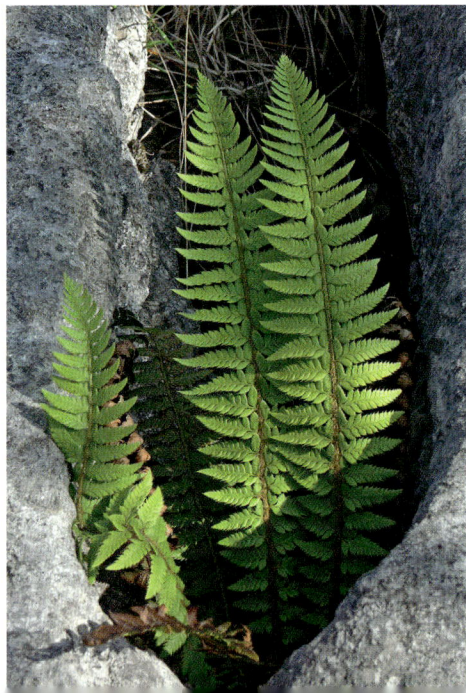

Above: Hart's tongue fern (Asplenium scolopendrium)

Below left: The hard shield fern (Polystichum aculeatum)

The **Limestone Fern** *(Gymnocarpium robertianum)* is a real gryke specialist. It is of modest size, but its bipinnate fronds (the leaf is divided into pinnae, which are again divided) open wide and flat to offer the maximum surface area to the sunlight.

The other gryke specialist, the **Rigid Buckler Fern** *(Dryopteris submontana)*, has paler grey-green bipinnate fronds arranged on brown stems. It is rare, and only found in the north-west of England and a few locations in Scotland.

Another widespread fern, but more of a limestone specialist found in grykes is the **Hard Shield Fern** *(Polystichum aculeatum)*. This has glossy, rather stiff dark-green fronds which are bipinnate.

The **Hart's Tongue Fern** *(Asplenium scolopendrium)* is common throughout the British Isles and is easily recognisable by its feather-shaped fronds that do not divide. It is also evergreen, unlike most ferns whose foliage dies away in the winter.

FLOWERS OF THE LIMESTONE UPLANDS

Baneberry *(Actaea spicata)* see p91, also known as herb christopher, is a scarce flower of upland limestone pavement, only occurring across a narrow band of limestone in northern England. It produces spikes of white flowers with a whorl of white stamens in the early summer, which turn into black berries following fertilisation. It is poisonous, potentially paralysing the heart muscles, but has been used as a homeopathic remedy, presumably in very small doses!

Bloody Cranesbill *(Geranium sanguineum)*: This rugged herb with its vibrant magenta flowers can be found in grasslands during the high summer, but it is a specialist of rocky locations to the extent that it can seem to be sitting on bare rock. It can find anchorage in very thin limestone, soil or in any organic material, such as algae, that has built up on the rock: it is one of the plants that initiates the build-up of soil. In the Pennines, it is found in the rugged woods of the Wye Valley SSSI in Derbyshire, but more widely in the Yorkshire Dales where it colonises the bare limestone pavements and cliff ledges. Its alarming name derives from the colour of its stems and its autumn leaves, which are red, rather than from the flowers.

Jacob's Ladder *(Polemonium caerulescens)* is found among limestone crags throughout the Pennines. At Malham, John Ray described finding it as long ago as 1671.

The **Alpine Cinquefoil** *(Potentilla crantzii)* is a rare herb that colonises rock ledges on cliffs and hills. It spreads over a rock face and produces tall stems each with a bright yellow flower which resembles a buttercup, but with five flatter petals. It occurs in Wharfedale and Upper Teesdale, but is not easy to find.

Lily of the Valley *(Convallaria majalis)*, see right, growing in a limestone gryke, is more associated with ancient woods and sandy, acidic soils; however it likes the dry conditions of a limestone pavement and here has some cover from a tree canopy.

Above left: Bloody cranesbill; (right) Alpine cinquefoil

Above: Jacob's ladder

Below: Lily of the valley in a gryke

FLOWERS OF UPPER TEESDALE

The geology and remoteness of Upper Teesdale supports a group of extremely rare flowers some of which, it is believed, have survived from the last Ice Age. These have become so rare due largely to changes in grazing practices.

Possibly the loveliest is the **Spring Gentian** (*Gentiana verna*) which occurs nowhere else in Britain although, like many of the plants in this section, it is also found in the Burren in Ireland, another karst landscape. It flowers in April or May in Upper Teesdale, when it is not difficult to find as its deep blue flowers are unique in Britain and stand out against the turf. They can be seen gracing the edges of footpaths over Widdybank Fell.

The **Teesdale Violet** (*Viola rupestris*) flowers alongside the spring gentian but is much more difficult to find among the more common violets. It has a rather small, pale flower, with a downy stem and serrated, kidney-shaped leaves. Although it was once thought to be restricted to Teesdale, a handful of other locations have been discovered in the north of England including the lower slopes of Ingleborough.

Mountain Pansy (*Viola lutea*): In her wonderful book on British wild flowers Sarah Raven writes:

"One of the best wild-flower experiences I have had was in Upper Teesdale in May…. Once I had reached the sugar limestone proper, I could hardly put my foot down without squashing one of these exquisite flowers…. undoubtedly the most beautiful of our wild pansies…"

She goes on to explain that horticulturists have always failed to grow real mountain pansies (rather than hybrids) in gardens.

Mountain pansies are quite common in the northern British uplands. The flowers are normally yellow, but they are often tinged with blue or purple.

Spring gentian (Gentiana verna)

Teesdale violet (Viola rupestris)

Mountain pansies (Viola lutea)

Teesdale sandwort

Scottish asphodel

Alpine bistort

The **Teesdale Sandwort** *(Minuartia stricta)* is easy to overlook with its tiny flowers, and it is arguably one of our rarest plants. It has only ever been known to grow on Widdybank Fell in Britain (although it is also found in northern tundras and beaches up to the Arctic). Its alternative name is the bog stitchwort as it normally grows on damp flushes on the sugar limestone where it forms loose clumps, entwined in hummock-forming mosses.

The tallest stems are less than 10cm tall, and the white 5-petalled flowers, whose appearance can be fleeting, are just a couple of millimetres across.

Alpine Bartsia *(Bartsia alpina)* has an unusual dark purple flower which is fleshy and rather hairy. It likes damp places so has suffered from meadows being drained and is now found around flushes among the rocks in Upper Teesdale and on a few mountain ledges in Scotland.

The **Scottish Asphodel** *(Tofieldia pusilla)* is found on mountainsides in the Scottish Highlands and many of the sub-Arctic northern countries. Upper Teesdale is the only English location for this tiny member of the lily family where it grows in wet flushes. The entire plant is just a few centimetres tall and the flowers are about 3mm across.

Alpine Bistort *(Persicaria vivipara)* is a slow-growing plant with a spike of tiny white flowers that don't always open fully. It has underground rhizomes whose spreading means that the plants are often seen in groups. It is quite frequent in Upper Teesdale and is also found in the Pennines on the high moors above Wharfedale, but is rare elsewhere in Britain.

Wet flushes also support the **Marsh Lousewort** *(Pedicularis palustris)* which is quite distinctive, standing up to 60cm tall on an erect stem which branches so it

Alpine bartsia

Marsh lousewort

Yellow marsh saxifrage

develops a 'Christmas tree' shape. It produces deep pink flowers on each stem. It is 'hemiparasite', so although it photosynthesises, using chlorophyll, marsh lousewort also obtains some nutrients by feeding on the roots of a host plant. Marsh lousewort is usually found in the sort of species-rich wetlands that have been turned into farmland over many years, It occurs in several locations in the northern Pennines but is more common in the south and south-west of England, and much of Scotland.

The **Common Butterwort** (*Pinguicula vulgaris*) is another moisture-loving plant which has found a way to supplement what it achieves by photosynthesis, this time by being insectivorous. Its sticky leaves curl round insects that

Yellow Mountain Saxifrage (*Saxifraga aizoides*) grows slowly on wet, rocky flushes. It forms low creeping cushions of tiny leaves, producing bright yellow flowers in early spring. It is found on mountains through much of Europe, and in the Pennines it occurs on Ingleborough in the Yorkshire Dales and in Upper Teesdale.

Common butterwort

land on it, stimulated by their struggles. It bears solitary deep violet flowers, each on a long stalk. The common butterwort is also quite frequent in several locations north of Calderdale.

Yellow Marsh Saxifrage (*Saxifraga hirculus*) is now very rare in the UK. Upper Teesdale is the only location in England in which it is found in any numbers, although it is common in arctic latitudes. Its attractive yellow flower can resemble that of the buttercup so that it isn't easy to recognise it in a meadow. In fact, it was overlooked in a number of places until the Foot and Mouth epidemic of 2001 when sheep were removed from the fells and *Saxifraga hirculus* was allowed to grow to maturity, when it was found to be present in abundance.

Yellow mountain saxifrage

Alpine enchanter's nightshade

Globeflowers on a limestone grassland

Bird's-eye primrose

Alpine Enchanter's Nightshade (*Circaea alpina*) is found among the wet rocks, high up on Cross Fell. In fact, it is not necessarily an alpine plant at all, as it is also found at sea level in Washington State and in other countries. It is uncommon in England, with a scattered distribution. It is partially parasitic on other plants but has proper green leaves that grow in opposing pairs and produces tiny white flowers.

The source of the river Tees is close to 800 metres altitude on the high slopes of Cross Fell, whose summit is wind-swept rock and has very little vegetation. However it is the biggest UK site for the woolly fringe-moss (*Racomitrium lanuginosum*), which is common in the arctic tundra, but rare in Britain.

LIMESTONE GRASSLANDS

Grasslands and unimproved wildflower meadows within the limestone areas can play host to a great variety of grasses and wild flowers, living on soils that are basic, neutral or acid and which can be boggy, wet or stony. In this section, we are discussing only a select group of limestone grassland specialists, leaving the many remaining species to Chapter 4.

Globeflower *(Trollius europaeus)* is a member of the buttercup family *(Ranunculacae)*, and its flower resembles a very large meadow buttercup, but about five times the size. They grow in cool, damp meadows, flushes and woods and can also colonise rocky ledges. Globeflowers are most prolific in the Dales and northern Pennines but also occur in the Derbyshire Peaks where they can look quite spectacular in numbers.

Flowering takes place between March and May, but in some conditions can extend into August. Pollination depends on insects which are capable of forcing their way through the many petals: these include certain bumblebees and moths and the chiastocheta fly, which feeds only on globeflowers. Following fertilisation, a dense cluster of black, wrinkled seeds are produced.

Bird's Eye Primrose *(Primula farinos)* is common in limestone flushes in the Yorkshire Dales but is only found in England from Yorkshire northwards. Its flowers appear in the late spring and are individually small, but form in a colourful spray atop a tall stem, so they stand out from any muted green background. Like other primroses, they are nectar-rich. The species name 'farinosa' means floury because the underside of the leaves (and the stems) look like they've been sprinkled with flour.

The **Grass of Parnassus** *(Parnassia palustris)*, also known as the 'bog star', was so named when it was found on the slopes of Mount Parnassus in Greece and, of course, it is not a grass at all, but a herb. It likes boggy places which are not acidic and has a wide distribution in northern Britain, although it has become quite rare. It is loved by many, to the extent that it is the county flower of Cumbria, even appearing in a stylised form on its flag.

One of the most typical summer flowers of limestone regions is the **Rock-rose** *(Helianthemum nummularium)* which can form large carpets of bright yellow flowers at lower altitudes. As its name suggests, it doesn't mind thin soil and rocky outcrops, and is pictured here on a steep slope in Upper Wharfedale, immediately below a small crag.

Grass of Parnassus

Rock-roses in Wharfedale

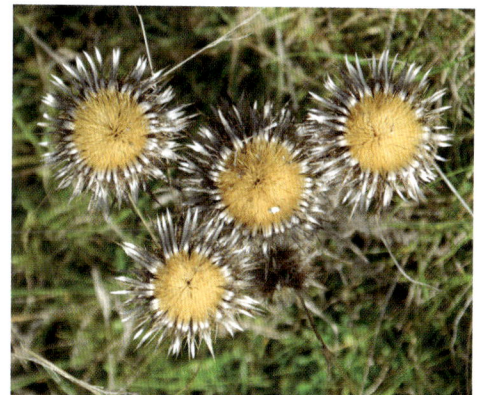

Carline thistles in Dovedale

The **Carline Thistle** (*Carlina vulgaris*) is a nectar-rich plant of the limestone grasslands, but in the Pennines is restricted to a number of unimproved areas of the Derbyshire Peak District. In full flower, it looks as though it has dried out, leaving only dead bracts and seeds, but is loved by butterflies and other insects for the nectar lying within its beige-coloured florets.

ORCHIDS IN LIMESTONE GRASSLANDS

In the United Kingdom, the majority of native orchids are found on limestone soils and this is certainly the case in the Pennines where they are frequently seen during the early summer months. Some, such as the pink spikes of common spotted, pyramidal or early purple orchids are quite common on many open untilled spaces. Others are exceedingly rare like the lady's slipper, or common, but not at all obvious because they are so small, or lacking colour, like the common twayblade.

Apart from the slipper orchid, British orchid flowers are quite small, especially when compared to the flamboyant tropical species. However, many have a delicate beauty, especially when the florets are viewed close up, and they often have an exotic biology: many have a symbiotic relationship with underground fungal 'roots' and some have developed bizarre strategies for achieving pollination. Orchids are yet another group of plants that has declined dramatically in recent times owing to loss of habitat.

The **Bee Orchid** (*Ophrys apifera*) lives on any dry limestone grassland, particularly in the southern half of Britain, but these lovely flowers are still found in lower

Burnt orchids

Bee orchid(single flower)

Bee orchid flowers on spike

Fly orchid

Lady's slipper orchid

grasslands of the southern Pennines. The flowers are large for a British orchid and up to nine occur, widely spaced, on each flower spike, of which there can be several in one small area of ground. The centre of each flower closely resembles a bee, but they are actually self-pollinating. They will flower one year then may not flower again in that location for several years.

In complete contrast, the **Burnt Orchid** *(Orchis ustulata)* is small and very scarce in Britain, found in a couple of Pennine sites, such as Aysgarth on the river Ure, and upper Wensleydale but is more prolific on limestone downs in southern England. This small orchid got its name from the slightly singed appearance of its flower spike, which appears from May, sometimes through to August. It is a slow developer, taking more than a decade to grow from seed to flower, which makes it exceedingly sensitive to agricultural practices. It likes short turf, so light grazing is very beneficial, but any agricultural treatment or disturbance will destroy it.

Like the bee orchid, **The Fly Orchid** *(Ophrys insectifera)* has single flowers arranged up a slender spike that can reach 60cm in height. The flower has evolved to resemble a small female wasp, a fact which is reflected in

the orchid's scientific name. The flower also emits a scent which resembles the pheremones produced by a female dagger wasp, attracting male wasps to it and assisting with self-fertilisation. Seen at close quarters, it is exquisitely beautiful with a burgundy velvet dress and a mirrored blue cummerbund.

It occurs in shady spots in open woodland and scrub, but can also be found in limestone pavements and grassland. Pennine locations include the White Peak in Derbyshire and, to a lesser extent, the Yorkshire Dales.

Also within the Yorkshire Dales is Britain's last remaining unequivocally wild group of the **Lady's Slipper Orchid** *(Cypripedium calceolus)*. The species was once more widespread, but was collected by enthusiasts, particularly in the nineteenth century. It also suffered through the loss of limestone woodlands until the UK population was almost entirely wiped out, although it remains widely distributed globally. The remaining truly wild British slipper orchids are heavily protected in a remote part of Wharfedale, but they can be seen at a number of locations taking part in a recovery programme through which seeds have been germinated at places within its former range. In Wharfedale, the orchid can be seen when it flowers in May, at the Kilnsey Flush SSSI, which is in the grounds of the Kilnsey Park Estate, alongside their commercial fly fishery.

Its maroon and yellow flowers are the largest of any British orchid, appearing on a tall flower spike up to 60cm in height. The plants are long-lived, but produce a limited number of seeds which rarely germinate, so any disturbance or change at their location could be critical to their survival.

Early Purple Orchids (*Orchis mascula*) seen here growing on grassland in the Yorkshire Dales. This is indeed one of the earliest flowering orchids and, although purple in this image, it is quite variable and can be close to white.

Green-winged Orchid (*Anacamptis morio*) is so called because the flower hood contains veins which are often green. It is also variable in colour, from purple to the palest pink. Green-winged orchids are not at all

Early purple orchids

common, but where they occur, such as at Leyburn Local Nature Reserve (Yorkshire Wildlife Trusts), there can be hundreds of plants.

Greater Butterfly Orchid (*Platanthera chlorantha*) is one of the taller British orchids and quite stately with its strong spike of luminous white flowers. It can be found in light woodland or grassland but isn't common in the Pennines. The scented Lesser Butterfly Orchid also grows in the Pennines and looks similar, but is smaller and more delicate.

Dark Red Helleborine (*Epipactis atrorubens*) grows in the Dales and the Peak District, producing maroon-coloured flowers on a tall spike in the summer. Helleborines are a type of orchid mostly occurring in woods, but it can be found also in rocky places and grassland.

The Frog Orchid (*Coeloglossum viride*) is an inconspicuous little green orchid that has a very patchy

Green-winged orchid

distribution throughout the British Isles. It occurs on grasslands, roadside verges, limestone pavements and rock ledges.

Another inconspicuous and rare species is the **Small White Orchid** (*Pseudorchis albida*). It is an upland species with closely-packed tiny green buds or white flowers clustered towards the top of the stem. In the Pennines, it can be found in pastures in Arkengarthdale.

A number of more common orchids found in the Pennines are the common spotted, pyramidal, fragrant and common twayblade.

Left: Greater butterfly orchid

Dark red helleborine

Frog orchid

PLANTS NEAR OLD MINE WORKINGS

Lead, along with zinc, iron, barium and Blue John (a form of fluorspar) were mined for centuries in the limestone regions of the Pennines because veins, or 'flats', of minerals were formed 290 million years ago where water in the limestone met hot granite which was pushing up from below and evaporated. The dissolved minerals crystallised, sometimes producing spectacular formations.

Mining, and the creation of end-products from the minerals, uses water from rivers which dissolves some of the released minerals and also carries large amounts of solid material back onto the surrounding land and into waterways. Many spoil heaps and open areas remain across the Pennine range, so the process continues, with very mixed results. Metal ions limit the range of plant species which can survive, radically changing the affected plant communities. However they also enable plants to grow that would otherwise be out-competed by more common species, creating a number of intriguing niches, several of which have been protected as SSSIs.

The following plants are those which can thrive in soils with a high mineral content.

Spring Sandwort *(Minuartia verna)* is also known as leadwort because it is so often found on the spoil heaps. It is a cushion-forming plant that can grow where there is very little soil (such as scree or pavement) and is very tolerant of heavy metals. Its prevalence on mine workings may be due also to

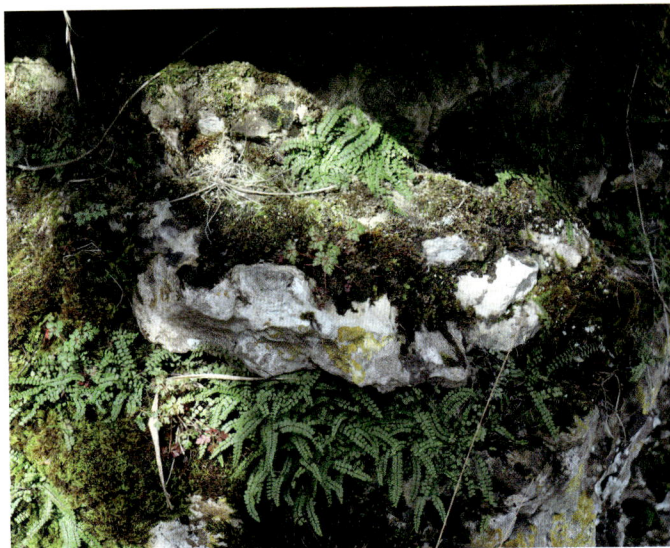
Maidenhair spleenwort on a limestone rock

Moonwort

the fact that there is little competition from other plants. It spreads across an area and when it produces its halo of rather large bell-shaped white flowers, the effect can be quite splendid.

Moonwort *(Botrychium lunaria)*, is an odd-looking little fern, only a few inches tall, that prefers well-drained sites, usually in open grasslands. It is tolerant of lead and other metals so colonises old mine workings in the Pennines and is a listed species in several such SSSIs.

Spring sandwort

Moonwort has had a reputation as a symbol of fertility, which is how it got its name (the moon being associated with monthly cycles etc). It was highly sought-after by medieval herbalists, some of whom believed that its leaves could open ways into the underworld as they resemble to a key. Another legend was that they could unshoe horses.

Other species typical of such areas are alpine penny-cress, mountain pansy and Pyrenean scurvy-grass.

Maidenhair Spleenwort (*Asplenium trichomanes*) see p104, is a small, rather distinctive fern whose fronds have distinctive opposing tiny leaves on thin stems which are almost black. It is not a limestone specialist, but grows in rocky places and is found commonly on limestone crags, and also on rocks in old mine workings. It is thriving on this crag above the river Wye in the White Peaks.

Limestone pavement in the Yorkshire Dales

Places to Find Limestone Upland Habitats

Limestone habitats are far better defined than heathlands and can be very distinctive and biologically rich. Starting in the south, the best limestone formations in the White Peak District are mostly along the river valleys, many of which can be readily accessed by footpaths, such as Dovedale and Monsal Dale. Winnats Pass is one of the best dry dales and has the spectacular Peveril Castle, Blue John mines and other caverns with easy public access.

One is spoilt for choice in the Yorkshire Dales as spectacular landscapes abound, but areas around Ingleton and the slopes of Ingleborough are easily accessed and include many karst formations, waterfalls, erratics and great views. Malham Cove is the largest limestone cliff in the UK and surrounded by beautiful landscape with fascinating features like Gordale Scar and Malham Tarn.

For Upper Teesdale limestone, waterfalls and rare flowers, the area of most interest runs from Newbiggin to Langdon Beck and the surrounding hills, particularly Cronkley Fell.

Limestone Upland SSSIs

SSSI Name	Approx Location	Hectares	Grid Reference
Tailbridge & High Dukerdale	West of Tan Hill	45000	NY 804050
Moor House	Upper Teesdale	38803	NY799358
Ingleborough	Skipton	5230	SD 760740
Malham Arncliffe	Malham	4934	SD 920676
Upper Wharfedale	Wharfedale	1123	SD 965735
Castleton	Castleton	624	SK 120820
The Wye Valley	Monsal Dale	593	SK 154722
Conistone Old Pasture	Wharfedale	297	SD990670
Bastow Wood	Grassington	128.6	SD 990657
Clough Woods	Darley Dale	119	SK 255615
Longstone Moor	Great Longstone	112	SK 195735
Coombs Dale	Stoney Middleton	93	SK 224744
Grass Wood	Wharfedale	88	SD 985655
Oughtershaw	between Wharfedale and Ribbleshead	76	SD 870810
Scoska Wood	Littondale	70	SD 915725
Stoney Middleton	Stoney Middleton dale	69	SK 210760
Strid Wood	River Wharfe near Bolton Abbey	59	SE 070560
Topley Pike & Deepdale	Wye Dale east of Buxton	50	SK 106724
River Ure Grasslands	River Ure around Aysgarth and downstream	46	SE 147870 – SE 157862
Kisdon Force Woods	East of Keld, Swaledale	38	NY 900009
Burnfoot	Tynedale	20	NY 689624
Muker Meadows	Swaledale	15.6	SD 914978
Freeholders Wood	Aysgarth, Wensleydale	14	SE 013889
Kettlewell Meadows	Wharfedale	12	SD 960734
Walden Meadows	In a high dale above Aysgarth	12	SE 005823
Yockenthwaite Meadows	Langstrothdale	11	SD 912786
Tideslow Rake	Tideswell	9.3	SK 152780
Wanlass Grasslands	Near Castle Bolton in Wensledydale	8.5	SE 065893; SE 054898
Ling Gill	East of Ribblehead	5	SD 801785
Beltingham	Tynedale	4.5	NY 783641
Len Pastures	Swaledale, below Gunnerside	4	SD 975968
Scar Closes, Kisdon	Between Keld and Thwaite	3.7	NY 893000
Cockerham Meadows	Near Grassington	2.5	SD998616
Far Mains Meadows	Wharfedale	2	SD 992628
Kilnsey Flush	Wharfedale	1.5	SD 972675
Lee Farm Meadow	Tideswell Moor	1.5	SK 131785
Williamston River Shingles	Tynedale	1.5	NY 681521

Farmed grassland in Swaledale, North Yorkshire

Opposite page: Yellow wagtail in a traditional pasture in the Dales

CHAPTER FOUR

Pennine Grasslands

Quite a lot has been said about grass in earlier chapters, from purple moor grass and mat grass in the heaths and bogs, to pastures and rare hay meadows in the Dales. Here we are looking at the wildlife habitats provided by those pastures and meadows, all of which are managed to some degree. In most cases, if the grass wasn't grazed or mown, it would be replaced by scrub within a few years and, in many cases, eventually become forest. The edible grasses that form meadows and pastures start being really viable

below 400 metres altitude, but do best below 200 metres. At lower altitudes moorland and heath can, and often have been, brought under management and made productive through drainage and fertilising until today very few 'unimproved' areas of grassland remain.

According to European and UK Government classification, the entire Pennine range is classed as a 'less favoured area' or LFA. This is a Europe-inspired classification of land designed to indicate where farmers are likely to need support to overcome difficult conditions and where abandonment might harm the economies and special character of the areas. The need to support rural economies and ways of life is often the driver to land improvement, trumping the existence of natural habitats which have existed for centuries or millennia.

The predominant landscape in the Derbyshire Peaks is green fields of grass separated by a network of grey limestone walls that spread for miles across the limestone plateau and where cattle, sheep or alpacas graze. A little higher up, the grassland gets rougher and only sheep crop the turf up to the altitudes where heather takes over. This pattern is repeated in the Yorkshire Dales, but in a bigger landscape where there are long stretches of open grassland in which management and grazing are less intense. Grassy fields also skirt the moorland and lower slopes in the millstone grit areas, but the Yorkshire walls here are darker and the ground is more likely to be boggy as water collects on the impervious ground-rock.

UK Government policy for LFAs has two prongs which at times can seem to be at odds with each other:

a) To ensure that livestock farming flourishes thereby helping to maintain viable rural communities

b) To conserve landscape and wildlife habitats.

Previous page: Yellow wagtail in a traditional pasture

Below: Mam Tor from the top of Winnats Pass: the boundary between the Light Peak and the Dark Peak

Above: Typical wild flower meadow flora in the summer. The dominant flower here is ox-eye daisy, with red clover, meadow buttercup and ribwort plantain. The grasses are red fescue and crested dogstail

Left: Silage field planted with ryegrass

*A lapwing on a patch of grass beside the Tan Hill Inn
with a stretch of white moor behind*

Rural community decline and agricultural land abandonment are serious concerns for the government, so grants have been provided to make the farming of marginal land more commercially viable. This, of course, addresses policy a., but on the face of it, ignores policy b., as increasing the yield of pastures involves fertilising the soil and replacing the natural sward with commercial, high-yielding seed mixtures dominated by ryegrass.

In order to protect the most threatened and precious species and habitats, selected areas have been given legal protection. However it is believed that between 1930 and 2017, 97 per cent of the flower meadows were lost. This has come about through the Second World War and its aftermath (the need to produce more of our own food), urban sprawl and infrastructure development, and changes in farming practices to increase farm yields and incomes. This seems to indicate that the balance between nature conservation and development is strongly tilted in one direction, to the detriment of our natural environment.

Richard Deverill, Director of the Royal Botanic Gardens at Kew writes in their online blog:

"British wildflowers are under threat and therefore so are the pollinators they feed. Not only is it heart-breaking to lose the beauty and colour these native flowers give the UK landscape, but the plight of pollinators has a very real impact on the food we eat ourselves."

Efforts are being made to redress the balance and a start has been made to restore meadows and diversity through Countryside Stewardship schemes through which farmers can obtain grants in exchange for working to promote wildlife interests alongside farming. Standards are also applied to the way that public bodies manage land so that the interests of wildlife are protected, for instance through guidance on protecting habitats for wild birds: (https://www.gov.uk/guidance/providing-and-protecting-habitat-for-wild-birds). However, the competing pressures of supporting rural economies, against the conservation and protection of disappearing wildlife, continue to vie with each other across the world and this tension is unlikely to go away. As things stand, it is the short-term human interests that usually prevail, at the cost of nature. Perhaps the greatest driver to altering this imbalance is to make people aware of the greater risk to humanity in the loss of pollinators: essentially, putting a value on 'natural capital' which could weigh on the decision-making balance.

Today, most land in the Pennines is protected to varying extents through legislation by being in a national park, a European Special Area of Conservation (SAC) or Special Protection Area (SPA), or a Site of Special Scientific Interest (SSSI). There is also the landscape conservation designation of Area of Outstanding Natural Beauty (AONB). In addition, land may be protected if it is owned or managed by a Wildlife Trust and be designated as a local nature reserve (LNR) or by another voluntary conservation body such as the RSPB.

In fact, in the Pennines, many of these designations overlap geographically because so much of the upland areas are protected. Whilst legal protection remains in place and is enforced, we can hope that the remaining wild flower meadows and unimproved pastures will survive into the future for us to enjoy. However, very little remains and the pressures do not go away, most pressingly from housing and infrastructure developments.

One great advantage of LNRs is that they depend on the enthusiasm of local people to protect and manage the land, where local interest is strong and active. However, the funding of nature reserves often comes from national or local government, so the security of both is dependent upon the policies, plans and whims of politicians, government officers and agencies.

Looking across most grasslands in the Pennines, especially they are grazed by sheep and cattle, the pasture is dominated by ryegrass and clover, which have been sown to replace the natural turf in the interests of agricultural productivity. The natural vegetation has been removed using weedkillers and the land fertilised and reseeded, a process that will have to continue, using farm muck, sewage sludge or chemicals along with weedkillers as deemed necessary.

The wild species that thrive in the nutrient-enriched conditions that surround farms and most settlements include nettles, docks, cleavers, dandelions and coarse grasses that are usually classed as undesirable by farmers. The native herbs and grasses that enrich wildflower meadows either cannot compete or cannot grow at all in these nutrient-enriched conditions. In addition, the diversity of wild animals is reduced, owing to the lack of food plants and the timing of sowing and reaping.

Of course, other wildlife does still frequent modern farms and settlements. Owls, jackdaws, swallows and stock doves often nest in agricultural buildings, and buzzards, gulls and crows will often home-in on a silage field as it is being cut, preying on injured or exposed creatures.

An example of wildlife adapting to human presence is a patch of grass around the Tan Hill Inn, at over 500 metres altitude, where lapwings calmly forage as people pass on the Pennine Way or come and go from the pub. However, those who seek wildlife and biodiversity in the grasslands will usually do best to look out for the nature reserves and less-managed places where nature goes its own way.

Wessenden valley in the northern Peak District

Golden plover among the pasture grasses

Traditional Management

Grasslands can be managed as meadows which are cut, or pastures which are grazed. The main product of meadows was hay, often combined with 'aftermath grazing' in which livestock would be put onto the area following mowing whilst the grass still grew. In the days before mechanisation, itinerant labourers went from farm to farm in late summer to make hay, reaping the high grass and flowers and leaving it to dry before storing in haystacks. It was then moved into barns to feed the livestock throughout winter. Candlemas Day (2nd February) was traditionally the halfway date when the farmer would check on how much hay was needed to get through the rest of the winter. Candlemas was therefore an important point in the annual cycle, and snowdrops, which were known as Candlemas Bells, were a marker of the time of year.

Livestock stay on pastures in summer, but on traditionally managed, low-intensity pastures, artificial fertilisers and weedkillers are not used and biodiversity is protected.

Disappearing Birds

In the twentieth century, mechanisation revolutionised farming. The first change was mechanised cutting with tractors rather than men with scythes, which caused **Corncrake** *(Crex crex)* populations to start declining. The bird was common and widespread in Britain in the nineteenth century but the harvesters were lethal as the birds were reluctant to break cover and would hide in long vegetation until every last bit was cut, so falling prey to the machines. When silage production became the norm from the late 1970s, their decline became catastrophic as silage is always cut during May when birds are nesting. This culminated in the once-abundant corncrakes becoming restricted to traditionally managed crofting land in the north of Scotland only. A number of other birds have suffered from the change to earlier cutting, including skylarks and curlews.

Another once common bird that nested in the Pennines is the **Yellow Wagtail** *(Motacilla flava)* which is now a rarity in the uplands where it nests in hay meadows but feeds in pastures (see page 109), often near rivers. Early cutting dates and a switch to silage have taken their toll, but fortunately the problem has been recognised: a scheme of special payments has been set up for farmers in the Yorkshire Dales and north Pennines in return for delaying the grass cutting until mid-July, to allow enough time for the young wagtails to fledge.

The biggest change to upland hay meadows was the introduction of silage during the 1970s. Silage is heavily fertilised so could take two or even three cuts a year compared with hay's single cut. Silage fields are often ploughed and reseeded with protein-rich rye grass so that they are, effectively, a crop without flowers. The cut grass is wrapped in polythene, even if the grass is not fully dry, removing potential food and cover for wildlife.

So it is that the balance between agricultural productivity and nature has been lost. The gentle cycle of springtime growth, summer flowering, late cutting, natural drying of hay in the open air helped by turning which allowed seeds to drop, harvesting and finally winter grazing has gone, unless supported by grants. Farmers cannot make a living in the modern world through traditional, slow, farming, whereas silage production makes farming commercially viable. The cost to the environment has been devastating, but there is now an increasing recognition of the long-term value of biodiversity to redress the balance.

A flower meadow in Wharfedale, full of buttercups and clover

PLANTS OF THE HAY MEADOWS AND PASTURES

Commonly found flowering plants which are specialists of the habitat are described below. Globeflower, grass of Parnassus, bird's-eye primrose and certain orchids which have been written about in Chapter 3 under Limestone Uplands are not included here.

The signal species of the northern hay meadows are wood cranesbill, melancholy thistle, yellow rattle and lady's mantle. These are often intermingled with, or dominated by, the more common meadow flowers such as ox-eye daisies, buttercups or clover. The grasses in these meadows are all common and widely distributed and their vigour, and value as animal feed, varies greatly according to the species, and their interaction with other plants in the vicinity.

Of course, the hay mown from a rich meadow is made up of all the variety of flowers as well as grass, but will seldom yield anything like a fertilised pasture sown with commercial seed.

GRASSES OF THE HAY MEADOWS AND PASTURES

Red Fescue (*Festuca rubra*) is a widespread grass species which is one of the most frequent grasses of unimproved traditional meadows. However, it is neither fast-growing nor highly nutritious, so is not favoured by farmers as feed. It spreads by rhizome and can form tufts or simply spread over an area if it is not mown. Because it copes with low soil fertility, it will also thrive on very thin limestone soils.

Crested Dogstail (*Cynosurus cristatus*) is another characteristic grass of unimproved meadows. It grows from seed, so mowing is not required to create the gaps in which fallen seeds can germinate. The leaves stay rather low, but the stems for its flowers and seed heads shoot up to 60cm.

Common Bent (*Agrostis capillaris*) a common widespread grass which thrives on poor soils and can grow almost anywhere. It spreads by rhizome and produces wispy seed heads which feel soft if you brush your hand through them.

Sweet Vernal-grass (*Anthoxanthum odoratum*) is usually the earliest grass to flower in a meadow, producing its spear-shaped flower heads in early to mid-April. These produce a lot of pollen which tends to provoke hay fever in humans. It has broad leaves for a grass which have a sweet smell of freshly cut hay owing to a substance in its foliage known as coumarin. These days, it is omitted from seed mixtures and often not favoured by farmers as it is not fast-growing and some livestock reject it when it is in their fodder. It is more of an upland species than those mentioned above and less of a generalist.

In spite of its name, **Yorkshire Fog** (*Holcus lanatus*) is not a Pennine specialist, but another ubiquitous grass of any moist piece of land. It is, however, one of the more attractive grasses, producing soft pinky-buff flower spikes in the early summer. Again, it not a favourite of cattle who leave the flowers completely alone.

Other meadow grasses include cock's-foot (*Dactylis glomerata*) and quaking grass (*Briza media*).

Sweet vernal grass

Yorkshire fog

WILD FLOWERS
OF THE HAY MEADOWS AND PASTURES

Some of the more specialist hay-meadow flowers are listed here, most of which can be found where fertilisers are not applied and where the ground remains undisturbed, including road verges and field edges as well as in meadows. The common flowers of the hay meadows and grasslands include meadow buttercups, bulbous buttercups, ox-eye daisies, red clover, which often produce intense swathes of colour in the springtime, along with ribwort plantain, thistles, scabious and knapweed. The image on p116 was taken at Kettlewell in Wharfedale in late May: it was one of many fields in the area which were full of all of these species.

Wood cranesbill (*Geranium sylvaticum*)**,** here growing alongside globeflowers, is common in the northern Yorkshire Dales but rare elsewhere in Britain. It is an important component of the upland hay meadows, where it can forms clumps of deep purple flowers which are a rich source of nectar.

Melancholy Thistle (*Cirsium heterophyllum*) is common in the Pennines and further north, but absent south of the Peak District. It has vivid purple flowers resembling small shaving brushes which grow in great colourful swathes frequented by many pollinating insects. Although it is a thistle, it has no spines at all.

Lady's Mantle (*Alchemilla vulgaris agg*) Lady's Mantle can be any one of about 15 species, or a hybrid of these: even the experts disagree about which are separate species. Two species (*A.glabra* and *A.xanthochlora*) are widespread in the Pennines, and around seven rare species can also be found. Each species varies in size, leaf shape and hairiness.

It is a rather inconspicuous plant of the upland pastures which occurs widely, but is particularly common in the Yorkshire Dales. It produces light green leaves,

Above: Globeflower and wood cranesbill

Below: Melancholy thistle

which resemble lily pads and are shaped to collect water, which they can absorb. In the summer months, sprays of tiny yellow or greenish flowers appear above the canopy of the plants. A closely related introduced species, *A.mollis*, is frequently found in gardens and also in the wild.

It is reputed to be useful in healing open wounds because of its high tannin content, but its Latin name, *Alchemilla* refers to an ancient belief that it could be used to turn base metals into gold, the alchemist's quest.

Great Burnet *(Sanguisorba officinalis)* has bright green foliage with serrated leaves arranged on tall upright stems supporting clusters of flowers which resemble maroon bumblebees. It is a rather useful plant as it is often planted where ground needs to be reclaimed or held together,

Great burnet

thanks to its tough and extensive root system. It is also used in herbal medicine to reduce bleeding and heal wounds.

Seeing **Harebells** *(Campanula rotundifolia)* trembling in the breeze on an open hillside is one of the summer treats in limestone country (although they tolerate quite a wide soil pH so can be seen in many Pennine locations). It prefers well-drained undisturbed soil so is a characteristic of the older, unfertilised grasslands and doesn't mind shallow soil. In the photograph, taken in the late afternoon, a Meadow Brown butterfly is resting on the plant.

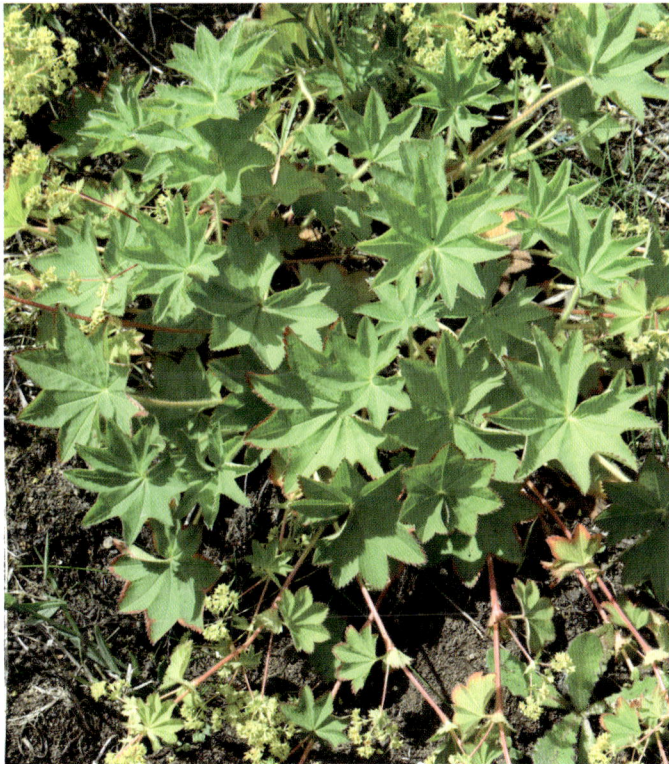
Alchemilla acutiloba (lady's mantle) at Darwen

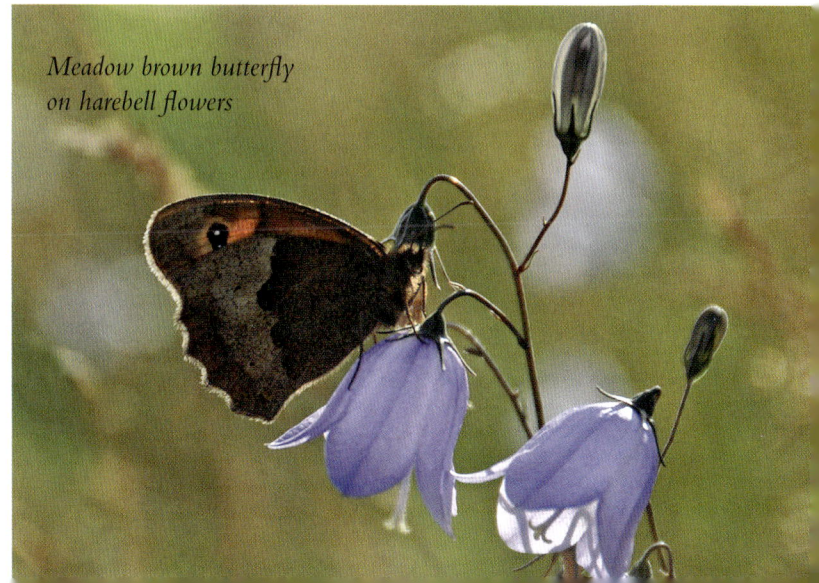
Meadow brown butterfly on harebell flowers

Wood cranesbill and a Buff-tailed bumblebee

Meadow Cranesbill (*Geranium pratense*) is more widely distributed than *G.sylvaticum* and found most commonly growing along roadsides, particularly where mowing is left until the later summer. It has pale rays on its petals which are there to attract insects, particularly bees, to its rich nectar store.

Yellow Rattle (*Rhinanthus minor*) is a very special plant in the wildflower meadows as it enhances the conditions for other wild flowers to thrive by moderating the growth of grasses. It is in of the family *Orobranchaceae*, most of which are parasitic on other plants through their root systems, extracting minerals and water for its own benefit. Yellow rattle parasitises meadow grasses and can reduce their growth, and therefore a farmer's yield, by 60 per cent or more according to one source. However, in doing so, it creates room for other herbs to flourish and cattle love it. If it is grazed or cut before it seeds, it will not reappear as it is an annual and can only grow from seed.

Yellow rattle is used in wildflower seed mixes for its habit of reducing vigorous grass growth and is best managed in meadows through delaying the start of grazing well into September to allow its seeds to spread.

Yellow rattle

A field of cuckoo flowers, or lady's smock, in west Yorkshire

Common Bistort *(Persicaria bistorta)* is a native flower, commonly used in flower borders in gardens, but its natural habitat is damp hay meadows, pastures and on road verges. It produces spikes, each one having a pink inflorescence like a bottle brush towards the top.

Bistort has traditionally been used to make Dock Pudding, otherwise known as Easterledge Pudding during Lent, which is quite bitter but supposed to be cleansing, so 'good for you'.

The seeds ripen within a calyx (cluster of sepals) which swell and dry, emitting a rattling sound when it waves in the breeze – hence its name.

The **Cuckoo Flower** *(Cardamine pratensis)* is commonly found in damp grasslands, meadows and lawns throughout the British Isles. The flowers can be white to pale pink or lilac and are produced on a tall stem from March to June. As it is an early flower and nectar-rich, it is important for insects early in the season, particularly the orange-tip and green-veined butterflies whose caterpillars feed on it. Its name is derived from its flowers being associated with the first time the cuckoo is heard to sing.

Common Milkwort *(Polygala vulgaris)* is a very small flower of short pastures and meadows, but it stands out because of its mainly deep blue-purple colour (although it can be white, pink or pale blue). It has a reputation for being good for helping milk production such that it was recommended as a remedy to help wet nurses nourish their infant charges.

Bistort in a meadow

*Comma butterfly
on a field scabious flower*

Tormentil flowers

Tormentil *(Potentilla erecta)* is usually recognised because it produces small bright yellow flowers with four petals during the summer months. The stems creep along the ground and produce glossy, dark green and deeply-toothed leaves. It is common across the UK in acid soils, often growing alongside heath bedstraw. It has been harvested to produce a red dye, known as Tormentil red, which can be obtained from its rhizomes.

Eyebright *(Euphrasia spp.)* is a hemi-parasitic member of the *Orobranchaceae* family, tapping grasses for nutrients and so limiting their growth. There are 21 species which are often difficult to tell apart, but the most prolific is common eyebright *(E.nemorosa)*. Eyebrights are often found in short chalk and limestone grasslands and meadows throughout Britain and Ireland.

Eyebright (Euphrasia nemorosa)

into quite a large spike of flowers in the right conditions. It is probably helped by having a more straightforward life cycle than most orchids and relatively hardy seeds.

Heath-Spotted Orchid *(Dactylorhiza maculata)* prefers damp places in good light. It is related to the much more prolific Common Spotted Orchid and its leaves have similar dark blotches. However the flower is quite different, with a wide, spreading lip and side lobes. It grows in damp places and favours acidic conditions.

Common Mouse-Ear *(Cerastium fontanum)* is a perennial with small hairy leaves that have a resemblance to mouse ears. It can sometimes form quite large mats on most kinds of soil and is very common and widespread in Britain. Its flowering shoots grow vertically to 40cm and bear small white flowers while non-flowering stems have a prostrate growth form.

Unfertilsed meadows tend to be full of flowers that are rich in nectar and loved by butterflies. The blue **Field Scabious** *(Knautia arvensis)* flowers are visited by a **Comma Butterfly** *(Polygonia c-album)* which needs the nectar during the summer to enable it to survive its winter hibernation. Both the butterfly and the flower occur throughout much of Britain, often on road verges and neglected areas.

Field scabious is a summer flower which has been used medicinally, particularly to help with skin conditions such as scabies.

Bird's-foot Trefoil *(Lotus corniculatus)* is one of the most common meadow flowers in Britain, which can form yellow carpets of flowers, usually on chalk or limestone soils. Where you find this plant, you will often also see common blue, brown argus or green hairstreak butterflies flying between plants and seeking their nectar. The **Pyramidal Orchid** *(Anacamptis pyramidalis)* is one of the more common orchids in England, its deep pink flower heads punctuating limey grasslands in the midsummer. It is typically triangular when it first emerges, but can grow

Above: The flower head of the pyramidal orchid
Top right: Heath-spotted orchid
Right: Common mouse-ear

INVERTEBRATES OF THE PENNINE GRASSLANDS

Upland grasslands and meadows are important habitats for many pollinators, including bees, the common butterflies and moths, along with many species of beetles, bugs, weevils, ants, bees, hoverflies, flies and gastropod molluscs. These are extremely varied and can be numerous, but are often little known; so in this section, descriptions are limited to the more obvious species of butterfly and moth that might be easily encountered.

Multiple meadow brown butterflies nectaring on creeping thistle

BUTTERFLIES AND MOTHS

One of the delights of walking through a healthy meadow in the summer months is to see butterflies dancing around the flowers and grasses, and it is still the case that, with the right conditions, they can rise in clouds as you walk. Many of the more common British butterflies are seen in the Pennine grasslands, particularly when the land is managed on a traditional basis, allowing the insects' entire lifecycles to complete. The majority of butterflies and moths overwinter in the larval, or caterpillar stage, some do so as pupae, eggs or hibernating adults. The **Speckled Wood** butterfly *(Pararge aegeria)* is unusual as it can overwinter as a caterpillar or a pupa. One significant problem is that insects overwintering as eggs or caterpillars are not easily found, being small, hidden, camouflaged or all three to avoid predation. This often results in their presence not being recognised when works are taking place so that entire colonies of butterflies can be obliterated because a landowner has decided to clear out a bit of woodland or scrub and no one, including the landowner, will ever know that the colony was there in the first place.

What we do know is that no butterflies thrive where monoculture rye grass is cut frequently and where insecticides are used. So again, the places to look for them will be traditional meadows and flower-rich road verges.

Meadows are more or less at rest during the winter months, and you have to know where to look to find signs of overwintering insects. The **Meadow Brown** *(Maniola jurtina)* overwinters in its larval (caterpillar) stage, and feeds on grasses throughout the winter months, only becoming torpid at the coldest times. The **Ringlet** *(Aphantopus hyperantus)* and **Small Heath** *(Coenonympha pamphilus)* caterpillars are less hardy, only feeding in milder weather during winter months, but otherwise hibernating. When the grasses start to grow in late March or early April, the larvae become active and feed voraciously until they are ready to go underground once more to pupate, hanging from the surrounding vegetation.

Speckled wood

Ringlet

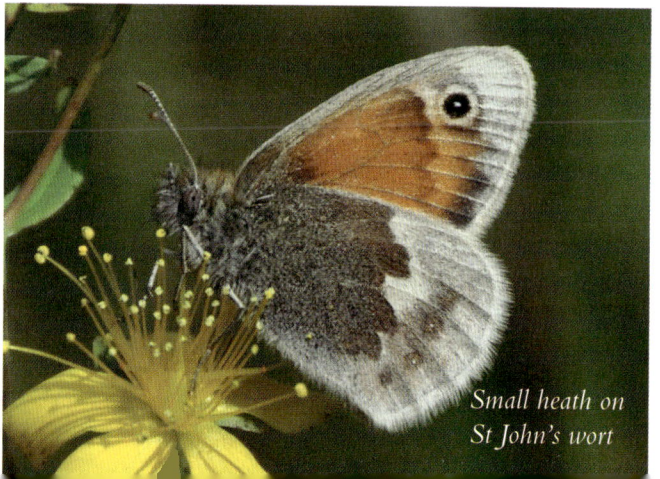
Small heath on St John's wort

Small tortoiseshell butterflies

Peacock

Male orange tip

Small Tortoiseshell (*Aglais urticae*) and **Peacock** (*Inachis io*) butterflies overwinter as adults and are often found around human habitation and farm buildings, rather than in flower meadows. This is because they, along with the migrant **Red Admiral** (*Vanessa atalanta*) need nettles to complete their life cycle and nettles require nutrient-rich soil which is best found where there are plenty of nutrients, such as from animal dung. The Small tortoiseshell also hibernates in buildings, so the field barns which are common on farms in the Yorkshire Dales are ideal. Peacocks prefer dark crevices and holes for hibernation which can be in trees or in walls, sheds and other buildings. They awaken with the first few warm days of spring when they emerge from hibernation to feed, mate and lay their eggs.

Orange-tip butterflies (*Anthocharis cardamines*) tend to be among the earliest to emerge from the chrysalis in the spring, closely followed by green-veined whites (*Pieris napi*). Orange-tips are quite common from April, preferring damp places often at the edge of woods or in neglected areas where flowers grow among the grasses. Both of these butterflies depend upon plants in the cabbage family, such as cuckoo flower (*Cardamine pratensis*) and garlic mustard (*Alliaria petiolata*) for their caterpillars to develop.

The summer is the season for butterflies and most do best when the weather is warm and dry, for which the Pennines are not renowned! Indeed, the number of any species of butterfly or moth seen during a season can vary dramatically, depending on conditions at critical times in their development as well as the availability of food sources for both adults and larvae.

The grass-feeding butterflies likely to be seen in Pennine grasslands are common throughout the UK, including the meadow brown, ringlet and small and large skippers. They are generalists, relying not just on a range of grasses but also taking advantage of nectar from many common wild flowers including knapweeds, clover, thistles, scabious, ragwort, various umbellifers in the meadows as well as brambles in hedgerows and road verges.

Holly blue

The **Small Heath** (*Coenonympha pamphilus*) caterpillar also feeds on a wide range of grasses, with a preference for sheep's fescue. The adult is rarely seen nectaring, so the picture on p125 of one feeding on St John's Wort is unusual for this species.

Wall Brown butterflies (*Lassiomata megera*) favour dry, rocky grasslands, often frequenting places where there is bare ground where they sun themselves with wings fully open. Their caterpillars feed on grasses like common bent and Yorkshire fog, but on the heaths, they will eat wavy-hair grass. Wall brown butterflies are occasionally mistaken for fritillaries, having similar colouration and patterning, but they are in a separate butterfly family. Wall browns only breed on unfertilised grasslands so numbers in the south have declined and they have disappeared entirely across the south-east.

Wall brown

Red admiral

The only blue-winged butterfly likely to be encountered in the Pennines is the **Common Blue** (*Polyommatus Icarus*) which can thrive on the limestone grasslands where rock-rose and bird's-foot trefoil are common. The male's wings and body are a lovely iridescent blue, but the female can be completely brown with orange spots, or partially blue. They are small enough to miss when they fly past, but they rest frequently and are worth looking out for.

Holly Blues (*Celastrina argiolus*) however are spreading into the hills, usually near gardens where their larval food plants grow (holly, ivy, snowberry, pyracantha). However they are occasionally attracted up to the moors in search of heather nectar. Their closed wing pattern is quite distinctive and, when open, their wings are a darker hue than the common blue, with black lines through the white wing-edges.

The **Northern Brown Argus** (*Aricia Artaxerxes*) is in the same family (lycenids) as the common and holly blues, and its size and shape are similar to the female

Common blues:
male in foreground and
female with wings closed

Large skipper

Northern brown argus:
upperwings (top)
underwings (below)

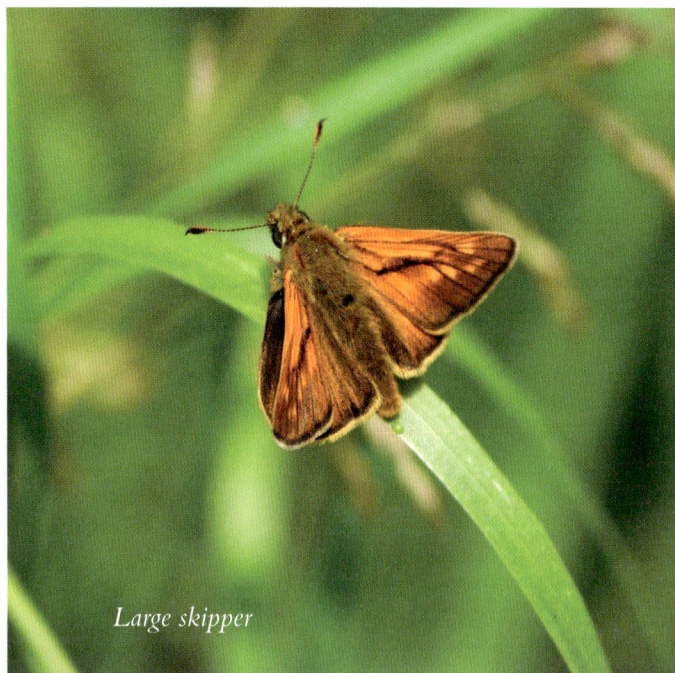
Scotch argus

common blue. Neither sex of the northern brown argus has any trace of blue colouration. It is an upland limestone butterfly which can occur in quite large colonies, always in association with the common rock-rose, which is its larval food plant. The closely-related brown argus (*Aricia agestis*) is very similar indeed to look at, but in the Pennines it is only found in the White Peak district in Derbyshire, being a more of a southern species.

The **Scotch Argus** (*Erebia aethiops*) is not related to the brown argus as it is one of the satyrids or brown butterflies. The name 'Argus' is applied to numerous animals with eyespots, and is derived from classical Greek legend. It is plentiful in Scotland but is one of very few butterflies that get more rare as you proceed south. It was long thought that it was found in only two sites in England, one of which is a limestone valley at Smardale in the north Pennines; however in recent years they have been found at a number of sites in limestone grasslands in the Yorkshire

Dark green fritillary

Wood tiger moth

Chimney sweeper moth

Narrow-bordered five-spot burnet

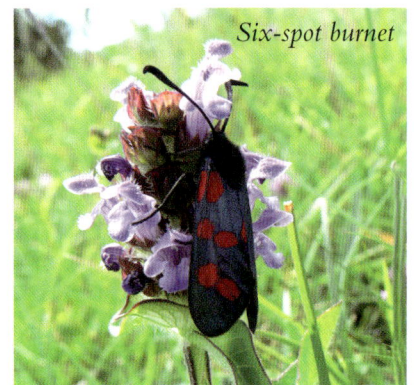

Six-spot burnet

Dales, after an absence of about a hundred years. They were once common in northern England, and in recent years, numbers may have benefitted from habitat restoration projects, and also from unofficial reintroductions. In Scotland their caterpillars feed on purple moor grass but in England they feed only on the rare limestone blue moor grass *(Sesleria caerulea)*, though the adults will nectar on a variety of flowers.

The **Dark Green Fritillary** *(Argynnis aglaja)* is a scarce species in the Pennines, thinly distributed in the limestone areas of the Yorkshire Dales and the Peak District where the caterpillars feed mainly on hairy violet *(Viola hirta)*. But they do wander widely and are occasionally encountered in the moorland areas well away from known breeding sites. At least one colony occurs on moorland in the south Pennines which is associated with a series of wet flushes where the caterpillars are thought to feed on marsh violets *(Viola palustris)*. They are powerful fliers and most likely to be seen on the wing during July and early August, but are easily confused with the northern eggar moth which they closely resemble on the wing, and which flies at the same time.

Alongside the butterflies, several species of day-flying moth are to be found during the summer, including the four illustrated here:

Wood tiger moth *(Parasemia plantaginis)*
Chimney sweeper moth *(Odezia atrata)*
Narrow-bordered five-spot burnet *(Zygaena lonicerae)*
Six-spot burnet *(Zygaena filipendulae)*

BIRDS OF THE PENNINE GRASSLANDS

The soaring song of the **Skylark** (*Alauda arvensis*) announces the spring across England, and hay meadows are the perfect habitat for them because they are left uncut whilst these ground-nesting birds are raising chicks. The vegetation in the springtime is at the right height and density for nesting and the diversity of plants attracts lots of insects upon which they feed. In past times, skylarks nested in spring-sown arable fields and grasslands where the crop was around ankle-height when they set up their nests and

Skylark on the ground

laid eggs, but to breed successfully, they need the crop to remain uncut until the end of June when the chicks have fledged. The change to autumn-sown cereals has reduced their range, although skylarks are still commonly heard around the Pennines.

The **Lapwing** (*Vanellus vanellus*) is a ground-nesting wader in the plover family. They are found in short grasslands especially where there are wet flushes and other damp places where they feed on insects and worms. Their nests are simple scrapes in the ground in a location where

Skylark taking off

Lapwing

the adults can look out for danger: if they feel endangered, they will take action to guard the nest, either attacking the threat or distracting it, and luring it away. Lapwings have distinctive large rounded wings which enable them to be very agile in flight, wheeling and soaring and emitting their distinctive cry.

Black Grouse (*Lyrurus tetrix*) are to be found in the north Pennines and the northern Yorkshire Dales. Unlike red grouse, they are a bird of the moorland edge, wandering between the moors, woodlands, pastures and hay meadows, according to which food is in season. In high summer the females frequent the hay meadows feeding on seeds of grasses, rushes and sedges, often accompanied by their chicks which feed on insects. As September approaches, they fly up onto the moors to feast on ripe bilberries in preparation for winter.

Black grouse perform ritual male displays known as leks, where many cocks compete to impress watching females between March and May. These usually take place in flat areas of short grassland where the males arrive at first light, well before the sunrise, and display vigorously for a few hours before flying off, or wandering a short way whilst keeping an eye on rivals. The most successful males

during the lek are able to mate with a disproportionate number of females.

Yellow Wagtail (*Motacilla flava flavissima*). The scientific name of this lovely bird means 'the most yellow of yellows', and the male certainly lives up to that, with his striking yellow breast and greenish-yellow upper parts. Females and juveniles have more muted colouring, with paler chests and greyish backs.

They arrive on their UK breeding grounds from early April, favouring damp habitats such as wet meadows, grazing marshes and river valleys for feeding. They usually

A female Black grouse in flight

move to hay meadows for nesting where they weave a cup out of grasses and line it with soft materials such as hair, wool or fur. Yellow wagtails are not common in the Pennines, but can be found in traditional hay meadows in the Yorkshire Dales and north Pennines.

Wheatears *(Oenanthe oenanthe)* are one of the earliest spring migrants to arrive in Britain, appearing in March having flown from overwintering in sub-Saharan Africa. They spend much of their lives on the ground and can be seen hopping along in open, rocky areas, in pastures and on heaths looking for beetles, caterpillars and small snails. They nest in crevices and holes in walls or rocks, or in old rabbit burrows where they line the interior with grass and other soft materials.

Wheatear

The name wheatear has nothing to do with wheat, but is a corruption of white arse, describing its most distinctive plumage feature.

Twite nest on moorland (see page 70), but feed their young entirely on seeds which they look for in local hay meadows during the summer months. Large volumes of seed are needed because it contains far less protein than insects and the reduction in arable farming in the Pennines has taken away the twite's most valuable winter food source, forcing it to migrate to the east coastal salt marshes. Between March and September, the main food species are dandelions, sorrel and hawkbit, for which hay meadows remain the best source.

Yellow wagtail in full song

A little owl in crevice in a field barn

The field barns and other stone structures in hay meadows provide nesting sites for a range of hole-nesting birds including **Jackdaws** *(Corvus monedula)*, **Stock doves** *(Columba oenas)* and house sparrows. Field barns are also good places to watch for little owls, barn owls and kestrels which may be seen perching as they shelter from the weather or simply using it as a look-out.

Pied Wagtails *(Motacilla alba)* are migrants commonly seen on grasslands throughout Britain. They nest in holes under the eaves of buildings, or in drystone walls and earth banks. They tend to favour short grass so are frequently found on lawns such as playing fields and golf courses, but the individual pictured was next to Malham Tarn. Swallows and martins also build their nests under the eaves of farm buildings.

Some grasslands can be quite wet if they are at a lakeside, or have flushes running through them and drainage is slow. Where pools form and there are muddy

A kestrel is ruffled by the wind in Millers Dale

Stock dove

Jackdaws on a limestone dale side

Pied wagtail

areas, wetland birds can be found which are more often associated with lowland marshes and estuaries.

Snipe (*Gallinago gallinago*) are wading birds that need damp ground, as their very long, straight bill is designed to search in soft ground for worms and insect larvae. They are a more typically upland bird than the lapwing, and are found on bogs, flushes and wet meadows.

Snipe are most active at dusk and dawn but are frustratingly elusive at other times. Their display starts with a loud repeated chip-per chip-per call, usually when perched on a wall or fence post, but sometimes also in flight. They also make a curious rhythmic sound during a display flight known as drumming: this humming noise is produced by air whizzing past the outer tail feathers with an additional vibrato brought about by the wings disrupting the air flow across the tail feathers.

The **Redshank** (*Tringa totanus*) is another wader which breeds on wet meadows and flushes in the Pennines but moves to estuaries for the winter. It has distinctive bright orange legs and a piercing, whistling call. Like the snipe, redshanks probe into the mud with their bills, looking for worms and leatherjackets which reside below the surface.

Curlews have been described in the Upland Heaths chapter, but they do breed on rough pastures and hay meadows as well, although if they attempt to nest in silage fields, their chicks are at risk from the huge mechanical harvesters.

Golden plover descend in flocks to feed on pastures, especially in March and April, from their nesting sites on the moors. If you see plovers, they are likely to be the day-feeding females, as the males feed at night-time and are on nest duty during daylight hours.

Redshank on a River Wharfe weir

Snipe on a post

Snipe in flight

FUNGI IN THE PENNINE GRASSLANDS

A number of well-known species of fungi typically grow on grasslands, including the field mushroom *(Agaricus campestris)*, horse mushroom *(Agaricus arvensis)* and the fairy-ring mushroom *(Marasmius oreades)* which are widespread in many improved as well as unimproved pastures around the country.

However, the most colourful grassland mushrooms are the waxcaps, or *Hygrophoracea*, many of which are to be found in the Pennines in the late summer and autumn.

The photograph above, taken on a grassy dale in the Peak District, has a **Pink Waxcap** *(Hygrocybe calyptriformis)* in the foreground and is included here to show the habitat as well as the specimen. It is a scarce mushroom that is also known as the 'Ballerina' because as it matures, the cap splits and curves upwards like a ballerina's tutu. It cannot cope with fertilisers so is restricted to old pastures that have not been agriculturally improved.

Overleaf is a collection of other waxcap species in the Pennines: scarlet waxcaps *(Hygrocybe coccinea)*, butter waxcaps *(Hygrocybe ceracea)*, the splendid waxcap *(Hygrocybe splendidissima)*, glutinous waxcaps *(Hygrocybe glutinipes)* blackening waxcap *(Hygrocybe conica)*.

A glutinous waxcap group

A blackening waxcap

A scarlet waxcap group

A butter waxcap group

A splendid waxcap

Where to find Pennine Grassland – see overleaf

A great deal of the Pennines is grassland, especially in the Yorkshire and Derbyshire Dales, but that is mostly improved pasture, and even unimproved pasture is heavily grazed so will tend to be species-poor. Unimproved grassland habitats that are not over-grazed are quite frequent in the higher parts of the Yorkshire Dales and the North Pennines. There are a few locations in Derbyshire that are reserves, the best of which may be Deepdale and Topley Pike managed by the Derbyshire Wildlife Trust. The National Trust own extensive grasslands at Ilam, Mam Tor and has acquired grassland habitats at High Fields near Longshaw and the farm at Greensides near Buxton.

Traditional hay meadows are to be found in the northern part of the Yorkshire Dales and the North Pennines, where there are more than anywhere else in England. The SSSI list overleaf will give the location of many of these.

Pennine Grassland SSSIs

SSSI Name	Approx Location	County	Area	Grid Reference
Birkdale, Gt Sleddale, Thwaite Common	Great Shunner Fell, west of Muker	N Yorks	45000	NY 856014
Malham Arncliffe	Malham	N Yorks	4934	SD 920676
Upper Wharfedale	Wharfedale	N Yorks	1123	SD 965735
Castleton	Castleton	Derbyshire	624	SK 120820
Bastow Wood	Grassington	N Yorks	128.6	SD 990657
Coombs Dale	Stoney Middleton	Derbyshire	93	SK 224744
Scoska Wood	Littondale	N Yorks	70	SD 915725
Ashes Pasture	Ribblesdale head	N Yorks	35.3	SD 776785
Muker Meadows	Swaledale	N Yorks	15.6	SD 914978
Harkes House Meadows	Near Keld in Swaledale	N Yorks	14	NY 860019
Kettlewell Meadows	Wharfedale	N Yorks	12	SD 960734
Walden Meadows	In a high dale above Aysgarth	N Yorks	12	SE 005823
Yockenthwaite Meadows	Langstrothdale	N Yorks	11	SD 912786
Fothering Holme	Arkengarthdale	N Yorks	10.3	NY 991040
Tideslow Rake	Tideswell	Derbyshire	9.3	SK 152780
Wanlass Grasslands	Nr Castle Bolton, Wensleydale	N Yorks	8.5	SE 065893
Waterfall Meadows	Between Eyam & Great Hucklow	Derbyshire	8.5	SK197772
Arkle Beck Meadows	Whaw, Arkengarthdale	N Yorks	8.4	NY 984041
Withens Clough	Above Mytholmroyd, Calderdale	W Yorks	7.4	SD 989234
Greenhow Pasture	Pateley Bridge	N Yorks	7.2	SE 118640
Park Hall Meadows	Healaugh in Swaledale	N Yorks	7	SD 035995
Oxlow Rake	Peak Forest	Derbyshire	5.5	SK 131805
Len Pastures	Swaledale, below Gunnerside	N Yorks	4	SD 975968
Scar Closes, Kisdon	Between Keld and Thwaite	N Yorks	3.7	NY 893000
Cockerham Meadows	Near Grassington	N Yorks	2.5	SD998616
Far Mains ....Meadows	Wharfedale	N Yorks	2	SD 992628
Lee Farm Meadow	Tideswell Moor	Derbyshire	1.5	SK 131785
Bradwell Meadows	Eastern outskirts of Bradwell	Derbyshire	0.9	SK 177807
Malham Arncliffe Cool Pasture	Malham	N Yorks		SD 967677

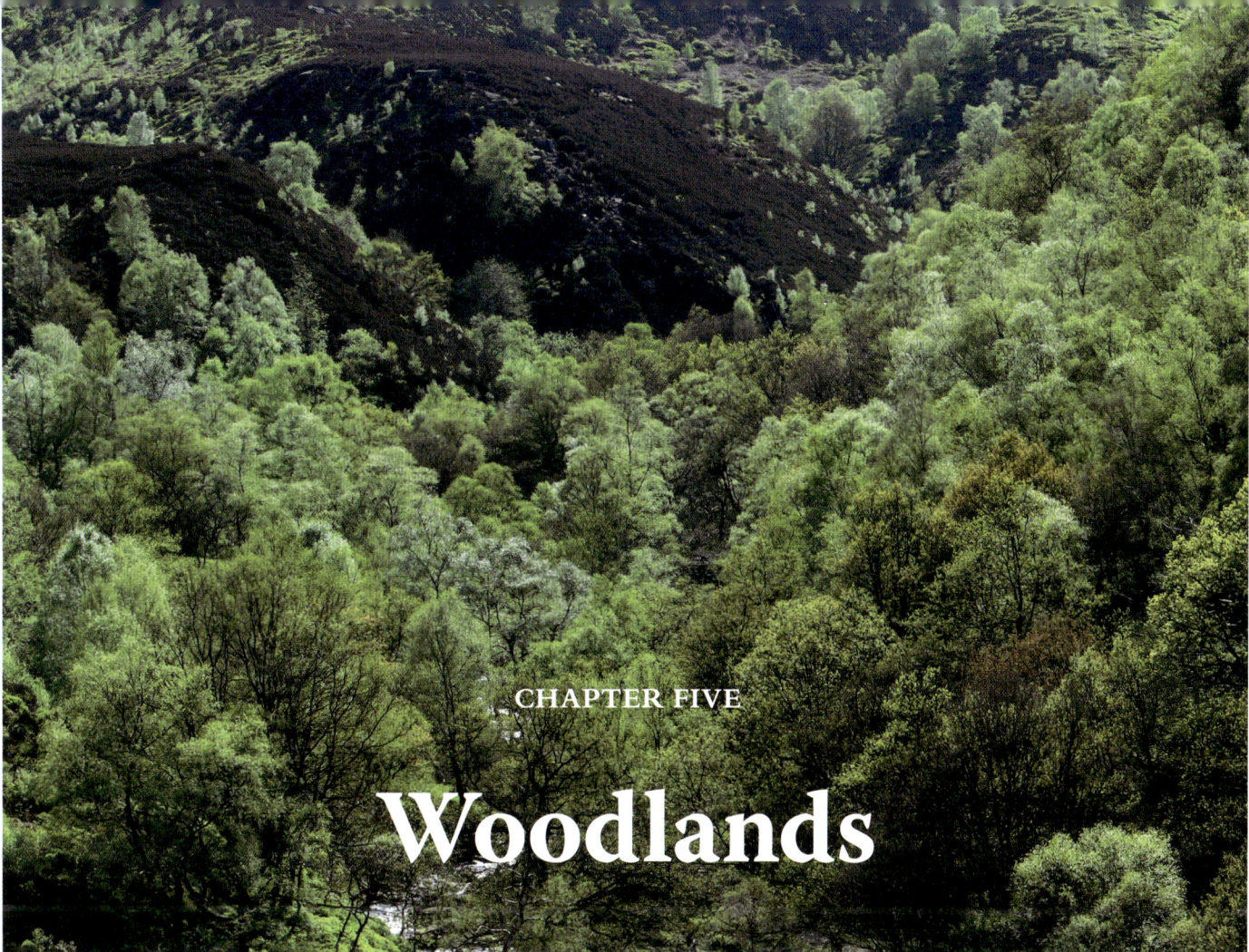

CHAPTER FIVE

Woodlands

The Pennine Hills are characterised by moorland and by grasslands and only a small proportion of the area is forested. Of that, little ancient woodland remains. There are areas where one may see quite a lot of woodland, mostly spread about the lower slopes of the hills, but almost all of it will have been planted in relatively recent times. The fossil record, particularly of pollen stored in the deep peat, tells us that 5,000 years ago it was very different. This was just at the start of the Bronze Age when the Pennines, along with most of Britain, was blanketed in a forest of predominately wych elm and Scots pine along with more open areas of oak and scrub. Alder would have dominated the lower, damper places. Interestingly, elm trees declined drastically across Europe over a four-year period at around that time, possibly due to an early equivalent of Dutch elm disease. This was also a time when human activity in the Pennines was increasing and forest was being cleared for cereal crops and grazing.

Above: Oak and birch clough in the West Yorkshire Pennines

Over the ensuing millennia, the decline in forests was relentless, with the wood being used for building, furniture, tools, fuel and in the agriculture and lead-mining industries. Where oak was cleared, it would be replaced by ash in many cases because its seeds germinate rapidly, taking quick advantage of the light and space.

The once extensive juniper scrub was cut down for agriculture, fuel (including for illegal liquor distillation as it produces little smoke), or succumbed to fungal disease.

Ancient woodland is defined as an area that has been wooded continuously since at least 1600 AD, which has not been replanted and has undisturbed soil, ground flora and fungi. They are valuable as stores of biodiversity and examples of ecosystems which have developed over millennia, so the biodiversity of these native woods can be extensive, forming a complex and occasionally mysterious web of life. In Britain most of the ancient woods have been lost and we are left only with remnants: fragments of the great forests that once defined the entire landscape. Where hardwood trees grew, particularly oak, the timber was regarded as much more valuable than the forest ecosystem (a fact that still jeopardises forests globally). And once trees were removed, the land could then be farmed.

Earlier plantations were often of beech, sycamore and larch which would have been planted on cleared ground, or replaced what was regarded at the time as 'inferior' woodland. A significant example is the mixed deciduous and coniferous woods around Bakewell and the Chatsworth Estate, where beech woods were planted in the 18th century during the creation of Chatsworth Park. Similar beech, sycamore and larch replacements have been planted through the years until now, in the 21st century, the landscape of the lower parts of the Pennine range is peppered with plantations of all sizes and with a tree species composition that may be entirely imported. Even so, there are few forests of any size in the Pennines: in fact, in the Yorkshire Dales National Park, they cover only 4 per cent of the land while ancient semi-natural woods cover only 0.78 per cent. The largest forests are all plantations, many established in the 20th century, including Langstrothdale Chase, Hamsterley Forest, the Derwent Valley at Ladybower Reservoir, and moorland to the east of the river Derwent in Derbyshire. These are largely composed of lodgepole pine, Norway spruce and sitka spruce, which are fast-growing soft wood trees planted as cash crops.

Most of the few remaining ancient natural woods lie where farming could not take place and where the timber was difficult to extract, such as on steep dale sides and along watercourses, predominately in the limestone areas. Old woods on limestone soils are defined by ash and hazel trees whilst oak and birch woods are characteristic of gritstone and wherever the soil tends to be more acid. There are some decent stretches of natural ash woods in the Peak District, particularly along the river Wye between Buxton and Ashford-in-the-Water as well as Lathkill Dale and Middleton Dale. In the Yorkshire Dales there is a valuable cluster of small ancient woods along the length of Wharfedale, most of which are designated as SSSIs. The

A view from Oughtershaw Side across to Langstrothdale Chase

Birch woodland on the slopes of Froggatt Edge

main species tend to include ash, hazel and small-leaved lime with hawthorn and wild cherry in the understorey and ferns, dog's mercury and wood rush on the floor. You are also likely to find carpets of bluebells, primroses, wood anenomes and celandines on the woodland floor in the spring.

Oak woods of any size are particularly rare in the Pennines, so although numerous small pockets of oak woodland occur, there are only three such SSSIs listed, none of which is extensive. The largest is the 59-acre Strid Wood on the Bolton Abbey Estate in the Yorkshire Dales National Park, while in the Peak District, only Bretton Clough near Hathersage and 26-acre Yarncliff Wood near Nether Padley remain. The SSSI citation says that Yarncliff Wood is a 'remnant of oak-birch woodland that once covered the edges of the gritstone uplands.' The main species in these woods tend to be sessile oak, downy- and

silver birch, with rowan, alder and bilberry in the understorey.

Some recovery of the ash-hazel and oak-birch woodland is happening in places where an industry has ceased and the land left alone, such as below Froggatt Edge in the Peak District. In addition, patches of birch and hawthorn scrub are to be found on many of the heaths, and there are places in the Yorkshire Dales where the flora typical of oak forest still survive among birch and hawthorn trees, but the oak trees are absent, having been felled. However, across the huge areas of Yorkshire moorland, trees are virtually absent and only a few small cloughs containing birch and oak remain.

Of course, apart from man-made plantations, woodlands cannot always readily be assigned to a particular type and, as with upland heaths, a mosaic of habitats often occurs so that ash, oak and alder woodland can all be found within quite a limited area. In addition, types of woodland are not always where you'd expect them to be: for instance the bedrock underlying the Clough Wood SSSI on the river Derwent around Darley Bridge is limestone, but landslips from the millstone grit above have deposited acid soils on which some ancient oak forest survives amongst a rich mixture of woodland and grassland types.

Because Pennine woodlands are so rare, many of the cloughs and dale woods have been protected as SSSIs and represent important stores of biodiversity. In part, this is because trees offer protection and shelter from the elements, but also because woodlands contain diverse habitats, including a tree canopy, trunks and boughs, the scrub and bushes forming an understorey and the forest floor where fallen wood and leaves rot down.

In contrast with native broad-leaved forests, the range of species in coniferous plantations will usually be far smaller owing to selective planting, poor light penetration and a needle-covered forest floor. It was a misguided UK government policy, following the Second World War, to establish coniferous plantations in order for the country to become less dependent on imported timber and paper. This resulted in the destruction of many ancient woods and the planting of coniferous forests in locations that were not always suitable. Many of the better-placed pine and larch plantations were established alongside reservoirs and close enough to roads and communities for them to have considerable amenity use for leisure and recreation, and they do provide habitats for plants and animals particularly in clearings and along rides, although their forest floors tend to be dark, rather barren places.

Some plantations, though, have been situated in remote locations where difficulty of access, combined with the poor quality of much of the timber, has resulted in a number of plantations being written off and left neglected because it is not cost-effective to fell and extract the wood. Such plantations can become impenetrable, but mature conifers provide plentiful cones containing seeds that sustain birds such as the siskin, redpoll and crossbill.

In any wood, large trees provide habitats, sustenance and shelter for a great number and variety of other creatures. They produce a great biomass of foliage, flowers and fruits each year which provides food and a place for invertebrates to lay eggs and, when leaves fall in the autumn, they are sustenance for the decomposers and their remaining nutrients are recycled. The boughs and twigs can be festooned with lichens or coated with algae, and provide roosts or escape routes. The countless invertebrates are, in turn, a major food source for birds and mammals, while crevices and holes are essential nesting sites. Even the roots contribute to the health of the ecosystem as they get invaded by mycorrhizal fungi in a complex symbiotic relationship that enables nutrients to be recycled. The recycling continues when all or part of the tree dies and falls to the ground and continues to provide food and shelter to a myriad of species as it decomposes.

In this chapter, the goal is to give the reader a general insight into the more typical or natural woodlands of the Pennines. Efforts have been made to include signal species and typical landscapes, although the space available dictates that much is left out: describing a single woodland habitat in detail would take up a whole book in its own right.

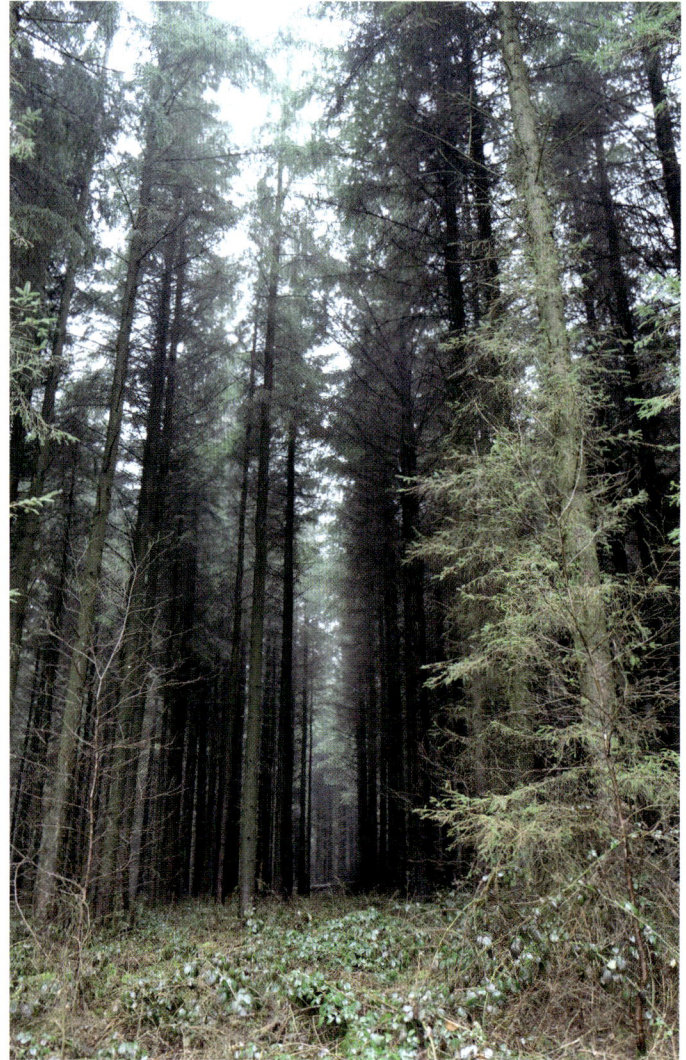

Coniferous pine plantation close to Langsett Reservoir in West Yorkshire

PLANTS IN THE LIMESTONE WOODLANDS

An ash wood on the river Wharfe at Langstrothdale

TREES

Ash trees (*Fraxinus excelsior)* most commonly dominate woods when limestone is the bedrock and ash makes up most of the upper canopy as one of the tallest native British trees. Rowan or mountain ash (*Sorbus aucuparia*), downy birch *(Betula pubescens)*, hazel (*Corylus avellana*), bird cherry *(Prunus padus)* and hawthorn (*Crataegus monogyna*) also characterise these woods but with canopies at a somewhat lower level, forming an understorey. Yew *(Taxus baccata)* and rock whitebeam *(Sorbus rupicola)* trees are characteristic of the precipitous gorges and rock outcrops which are

present in many limestone dales.

The image on page 146 shows Wain Wath Force in Upper Swaledale where the river Swale tumbles over a hard shelf of shale. There is a rowan tree on the left and a mixed woodland ascending the limestone cliff. There are wych elm along the lower slopes with ash and birch rising to the crags, where the deciduous species are joined by yew trees.

The land is not grazed so there is a rich variety of vegetation growing immediately above the river which includes reeds and sedges, grasses and ferns. Further into the trees, the understorey includes hawthorn, blackthorn and bird cherry.

The image on page 147 is taken from a few hundred metres further up the dale where the land has been cleared and enclosed for sheep farming. The effect is very attractive to the eye as the fells are opened up, but the river edges have few trees and only grass is growing.

This gives some idea of the dramatic alteration to the landscape that humans have brought about.

Wych Elm (*Ulmus glabra*) is our native species of elm, the 'English elm' (*Ulmus minor*) being actually a native of southern Europe). In spite of Dutch elm disease having wiped out virtually all of the mature elms in Great Britain, the wych elm remains quite common in limestone woodland, as well as in many copses and hedgerows. They do well in the limestone cloughs as they like steep, rocky ground, although they never reach maturity now. Prior to the disease, wych elms would have competed with the ash for space in the high canopy, but they now seldom grow above three or four metres in height before they are colonised by the beetles which carry the fungal pathogen,

Detail of an ash tree and foliage

Ophiostoma sp., that kills the tree, preventing further development. Apart from the tragic loss of a tree that graced much of the British countryside, this also resulted in the lovely white-letter hairstreak butterfly becoming scarce as it depends upon elm trees for breeding successfully.

Sycamore trees *(Acer pseudoplatanus)* are also present in most broad-leaved woods and many copses, either through chance seed falls or through being planted. They are a native of southern Europe, probably introduced to England in the Middle Ages.

Ash die-back. We now live with the fear that the future of these ash woods is under threat from 'chalara', or ash die-back disease which has entered the country from Europe and is spreading through our forests from the

Wain Wath Force in Upper Swaledale showing the natural woodland which exists if ungrazed

The banks of the River Swale, treeless when grazed by sheep

One of the strangest associations is with a rare and inconspicuous orchid of the deep woods: this is the **Birds-nest Orchid** *(Neottia nidus-avis)* which is beige and non-photosynthesising but depends on its symbiotic fungae for its survival. One is unlikely to find these orchids unless one is looking for them, and their occurance in Pennine woods is rare, but they are mentioned here as an intriguing curiosity.

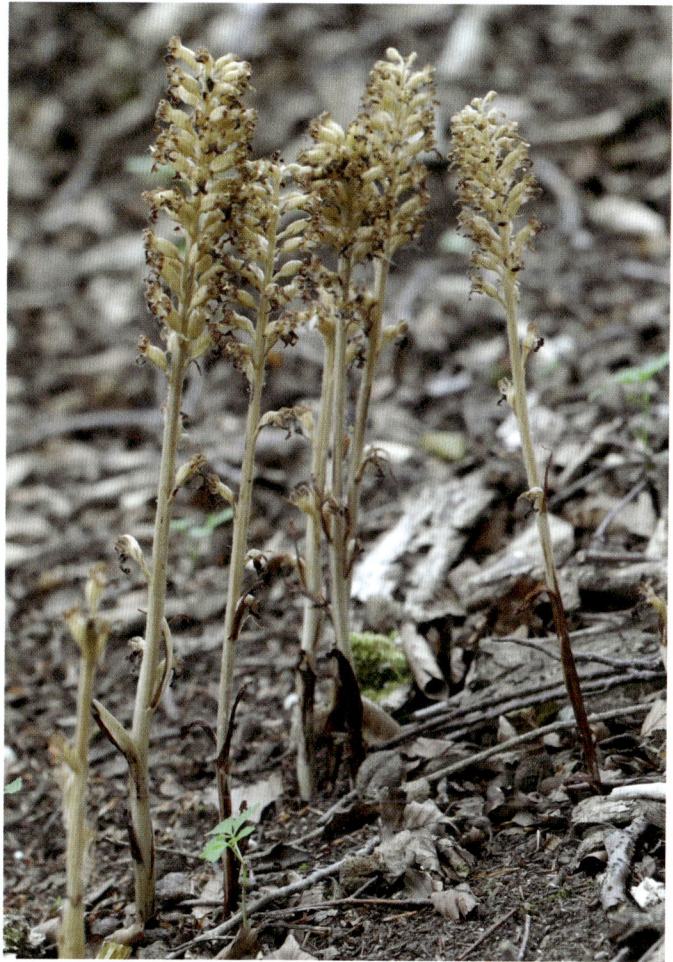

south of England. Chalara is a fungal disease of ash trees caused by *Hymenoscyphus fraxineus* which spreads mostly by wind-blown spores. Mature trees seem to be able to withstand infection better than young trees, almost all of which die, apart from a few that seem to be immune. Research continues into the genetics that brings about this immunity, but there is some optimism that ash woodlands will recover with time as seedlings of the immune trees grow.

Fungi play a huge role in forests, although it is true that they can spread disease where trees are not resistant to it. Our British forests thrive alongside honey fungus and many other mushrooms that are potentially lethal, but trees and fungi also depend upon each other and are both part of a healthy ecosystem.

Fungi form symbiotic relationships with many woodland plants through penetrating their root systems and sharing nutrients: which organism benefits the most from this varies of course.

Birds-nest orchids

FUNGI IN THE PENNINE WOODLANDS

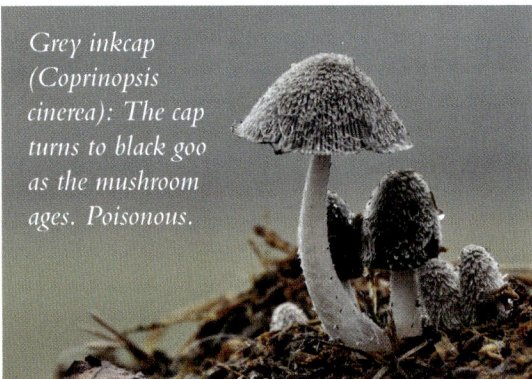

Grey inkcap (Coprinopsis cinerea): The cap turns to black goo as the mushroom ages. Poisonous.

Beneath the surface of an established forest floor the soil can be laced with fungal threads called mycelium which may belong to many different species. If it is a mycorrhizal species the mycelium forms a symbiotic relationship with trees which assists in nutrient uptake by the tree roots. Below are the fruiting bodies (ie mushrooms) of six woodland species, each representing a fungal group (Amanitas, Inkcaps, Bonnets, Boletes, Saddles and Cups). All were photographed in the Peak District. (NB these are not particular to limestone regions.)

Above: Fly agaric (Amanita muscari): White gills and spores. Poisonous

Bay bolete (Boletus badius): Large fungi with pores, not gills, edible

Clustered bonnet (Mycena inclanata): Small, 'pixie bonnet' shape with a slender stipe

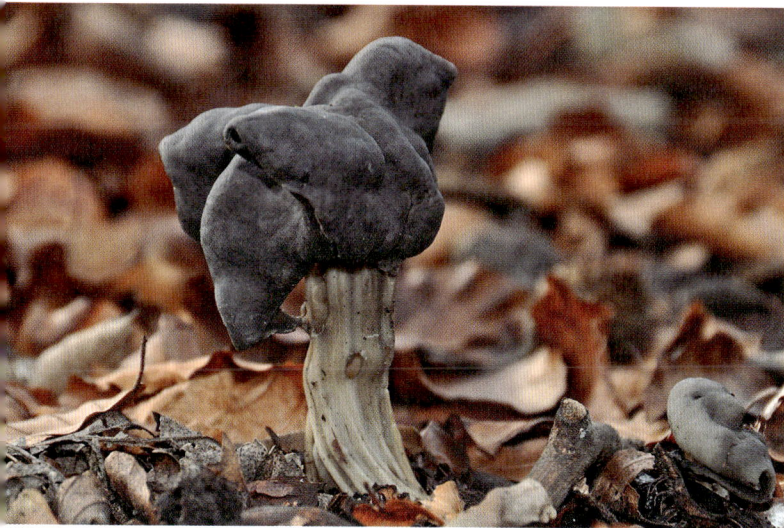

Elfin saddle (Helvella lacunosa): Spores borne on the cap surface: no gills or pores

Blistered cup (Peziza vesiculosa): Cup-shaped fungi with no stem and thin flesh

OTHER PLANTS OF THE LIMESTONE WOODLANDS

The richest woods for biodiversity tend to be ancient, and in the springtime they come into their own. As the days lengthen and the temperature rises, the wood turns from a place of browns and greys, bare branches and leaf litter, to a riot of burgeoning buds and colourful flowers. This is because many woodland flowers rush to bloom in the early spring, before the tree leaves open and take most of the sunlight. They are mostly not limestone specialists, but will be encountered in many woods, especially where the ground is undisturbed.

Bluebells *(Hyacinthoides non-scripta)* often carpet the forest floor in a scented amethyst carpet while the pristine white stars of wood anemones and the bright yellow lesser celandines cluster in smaller mats. In some of the wetter places in the Peak District, golden saxifrage *(Chrysosplenium oppositifolium)* can be among the earliest to flower, carpeting

Above: An off-shoot of Middleton Dale, below Eyam in Derbyshire in April, where the forest floor is carpeted with golden saxifrage on the left and ramsons along the beck on the right.

the valley floor in green and yellow. A bit later, greater stitchworts *(Stellaria holostea)* mingle with the bluebells and primroses *(Primula vulgaris)* often lining the banks and sides of footpaths. Also in the spring, the entire forest floor can be covered in wild garlic or ramsons *(Allium ursinum)*, their delicate white blossoms at odds with their heavy garlicky aroma.

Top Left: Wood anenomes (Anenome nemorosa) on the banks of the Derwent in Monsal Dale
Top Right: A swathe of primroses and anenomes
Lower Left: Bluebells frequently carpet the forest floor in April
Lower Right: Wood sorrel (Oxalis acetosella) grows in the damper places, sometimes in deep shade among the mosses. It has clover-like 3-lobed leaves which taste of sour apple. The flowers are delicate and very pretty, with white petals streaked with pale lilac veins, but they do not produce much seed. Later on, in midsummer, there is a second flowering in which the leaves never open, but self-pollinate and from which most viable seeds are produced. Wood sorrel leaves anticipate rain by folding up and they remain closed until the rain has stopped.

Moschatel flowers

Moschatel *(Adoxa moschatellina)* is another early flowering plant of the damp forest floor. It has little distinguishing colour, being greenish to white and exudes a musky scent which attracts pollinating insects. (Moschata is the Greek word for musk.) It is a low-growing plant of old woodlands.

Another name for moschatel is town hall clock, because each flower has four faces at right angles to each other, each with five green petals, and a four-petal upward-facing 'roof'.

It seems imperative to mention two woodland plants with a fairly universal distribution here as any visitor to Pennine woods is likely to come across them.

Mezereon *(Daphne mezereum)* is often found in gardens but is thought to be truly native in the limestone woodlands of the Pennines where the adjacent photo was taken in the Peak District. It is a deciduous shrub which can be 1.5 m tall. The pink-to-purple flowers have a strong

scent and appear on the bare stems in March, before the leaves appear. The bright red berries are very poisonous for humans, but not for fruit-eating birds such as thrushes, who spread the seeds in their droppings.

The leaves and twigs are also poisonous and simply touching them can cause a skin rash. Its sap was once used as a cosmetic to add colour to the cheeks by causing a facial skin rash. This isn't especially attractive, and burst blood vessels were an outcome so the idea was soon dropped.

Also poisonous, but fairly ubiquitous, especially in limestone woodlands, is **Dog's Mercury** *(Mercurialis perennis)*. This dull green plant with rather colourless flowers is very poisonous. It is an ancient woodland indicator, carpeting the forest floor, spreading rapidly through

Mezereon

Dog's mercury in a hazel coppice woodland in Wharfedale

underground rhizomes. It is found on many woodland floors and also on crags and undisturbed banks, but in the hazel coppice in Wharfedale above, it has truly taken over.

In the later spring, the spectacular flower carpets fade away as the canopy of leaves above takes the light and the flowers that remain are mostly along rides and clearings. The most frequent forest floor plants are widespread across the country, including dog's mercury, wood avens *(Geum urbanum)*, brambles *(Rubus fruticosus)*, ivy *(Hedera helix)*, and grasses, along with ferns: male fern, limestone fern, holly fern, hart's tongue fern and the ubiquitous bracken. Brambles and ivy have great importance as food plants for insects and birds, so that in early summer, a thorny bramble thicket can be alive with butterflies and from August, the ivy flower provides abundant nectar and pollen when almost all other flowers have finished.

Honeysuckle *(Lonicera perclymenum)* is a welcome summer flower, occasionally found climbing up the smaller forest trees and, in a few of the oldest woods, drifts of lily-of-the-valley *(Convallaria majalis)* can grace the forest floor, charming the senses with its sweet vanilla scent.

A number of more or less inconspicuous forest floor species can be encountered in the limestone woods, especially in the lower reaches of the Pennines.

Herb Paris *(Paris quadrifolia)* often grows in patches among the ubiquitous dog's mercury, so it can be tricky to spot as their foliage is similar in colour.

Solomon's-seal *(Polygonatum multi-florum)* has arching stems with pairs of large, dark green leaves with waxy-blue undersides with ribs that fan out from the stem. Clusters of small greenish-white flowers appear in the early summer, hanging like little bells.

The **Mountain Currant** *(Ribes alpinum)* is a calcareous woodland shrub that is only found at altitude and is scarce in western Europe, confined to a few northern sites in England and Wales. It can be low-lying and trail over rocky outcrops or form thickets. It has separate male and female plants, the female producing clusters of red berries after flowering, which have a watery taste.

The plants that grow on the thin soils on rocky outcrops and steep scree-covered slopes which pepper the Pennine woodlands tend to be grasses like wood melick *(Melica uniflora)* and false brome *(Brachypodium sylvaticum)* along with the less spectacular herbs, such as wood sage *(Teucrium scorodonia)* and dog's mercury.

Honeysuckle

Herb paris and (below) Mountain currant

This limestone pinnacle in Dovedale rises from a scrubby ash wood, festooned with grasses and young trees growing from within the cracks in the rock.

As most of the limestone woods are in river valleys where water collects on its way down to the stream, so the ground and rocks are almost always damp or running with water. These are the perfect conditions for mosses which coat every available surface.

These are not the sphagnum mosses of the open moors, but species that form mats on trees, rocks and cliffs, where water drips from them rather than collecting as it does on the blanket bogs. The image below shows mosses carpeting rocks in Middletondale in the White Peak District. There is also a large hart's tongue fern and a couple of ramson plants.

Right: A limestone pinnacle on the river Dove

Below: Moss and hart's tongue fern by water

PLANTS IN THE GRITSTONE WOODLANDS

Where the underlying rock is millstone grit, the soil tends to be acid or neutral and the dominant trees in the native woods and copses are sessile oak along with downy and silver birch. If conditions are not too wet and boggy, many of the plants already mentioned, which are not limestone specialists, can occur. Carpets of flowers are less commonly encountered, although bluebells can do well, along with golden saxifrage in occasional wet areas and foxgloves (*Digitalis purpurea*) which are often found in the drier glades and clearings in the summer.

The flowering plants that most often carpet the forest floor in gritstone woodlands are greater wood rush, bilberry and wavy hair grass with bramble at lower altitudes. In some places, ferns will predominate, with bracken on drier soil and broad buckler-, male-, lady- and hart's-tongue ferns in wetter locations. Where water off the high moors and blanket bogs collects, the vegetation can become more similar to that of the bogs so that heather and bilberry thrive on the forest floor, often with sphagnum moss between the plants.

Many species of mosses and lichens colonise any available surface on the forest floor and may form a colourful layer on the trunks and boughs of the trees. A rich fungus flora also occurs in older woods.

Above: Bilberry bushes carpeting a birch wood floor

Right: Great wood-rush carpeting the forest floor in West Yorkshire

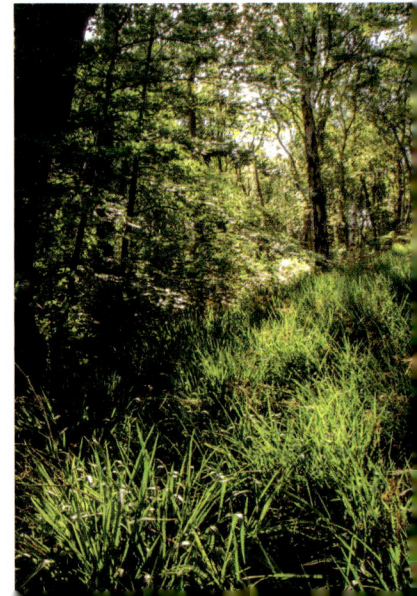

INVERTEBRATES IN THE PENNINE WOODLANDS

All forests contain a myriad of invertebrates and depend on them for breaking down dead plant material, providing food for other animals and offering countless other functions. However, there is not space here to consider them in any meaningful way, so only a handful of the more noticeable examples are mentioned because they can add to the experience of being in a woodland. This does mean that we are ignoring the great biomass of aphids, beetles, bugs, spiders, worms and ants without which a forest ecosystem could not function other than as a sterile parkland, but we hope that this will not detract from conveying the main characteristics of woodland habitats.

In the springtime the orange tip and the green-veined white butterflies can be seen along the flowery rides and clearings, seeking nectar or somewhere to lay their eggs, or just fluttering in a shaft of warm sunlight. Orange tip females have to take extra care with their choice of plants, because the caterpillars are cannibalistic, and will eat any butterfly eggs or smaller caterpillars which they encounter. They have therefore adapted to avoid plants on which orange tip eggs have been laid.

The **Speckled Wood** butterfly (*Pararge aegeria*) flies in wooded places from April to October and is one of the few species that has increased in numbers and territory in recent decades. They will often be seen basking with open wings in sunny spots, such as footpaths. Males rise up to intercept a potential mate or an intruding male and engage in prolonged, aerial spirals.

Orange tip on a bluebell flower

Speckled wood

Above: Purple hairstreak butterfly

Below: White-letter hairstreak butterfly

The **Purple Hairstreak** *(Favonius quercus)* normally lives high up in the foliage of oak trees from which they seldom stray and, unlike the speckled wood, never basks on the ground. They often occur in quite large colonies and may be seen flitting about the leaves and branches of woodland oaks from the second half of July. They rarely visit flowers, getting most of their sugar from aphid honeydew on leaves. Being small canopy dwellers that rarely open their wings when at rest, they merge into the leafy background, but when a purple hairstreak does open its wings, it reveals a flash of iridescent purple which is worth looking for. They seem more likely to be active and to visit lower roosts in the early evening.

The **White-letter Hairstreak** *(Satyrium w-album)* is another treetop dweller that consumes honeydew on oak and ash trees. They do descend to human level more than their purple cousin, however, and can occasionally be found on creeping thistle and other nectar-rich flowers on woodland edges and rides. The white-letter hairstreak depends on elm trees exclusively for breeding, so its numbers nationally plummeted following Dutch elm disease. Eggs are laid in crevices in wych elm bark in the summer, which hatch when the buds are swelling in the following March. The caterpillar feeds on the buds and flowers until ready to form a chrysalis. They live in small colonies, staying quite close to their breeding site.

Other butterflies that fly in these woods tend to be grassland or widespread species that seek out food plants along forest rides and woodland edges. These can include ringlets, meadow browns, green-veined whites and commas, which are all much easier to spot than the hairstreaks as they are considerably larger and live close to the ground.

Beetles make up 40% of the total of all insect species and many inhabit the woodlands. In spite of this, you have to look for them as they are normally hidden in dead and living trees, or under the leaf litter and stones on the ground. Some that have the greatest effect on woods are numerous, but never noticed, such as elm bark beetles in

the genus *Scolytus* which disseminate the fungus that causes Dutch elm disease. Others recycle animal remains, like sexton and dor beetles (see Chapter 2). Many feed on rotting wood on the ground or old wood in trees, including the larvae of the death-watch beetle *(Xestobium rufovillosum)*, stag beetle *(Lucanus cervus)* and rhinoceros beetle *(Sinodendron cylindricum)*. The adults of these species live in the trees, feeding on sap. Then there are carnivorous beetles, like the coach-horse beetle *(Staphulinus olens)* and vegetarian beetles like the chafers, and fungus-eating beetles like the false ladybird *(Endomychus coccineus)*.

If you come across a pile of soft-looking plant debris in a sunny position in a wood, check carefully before you are tempted to sit on it as it might be a **Northern (or hairy) Wood Ant** *(Formica lugubris)* nest. These are quite large ants which are highly social, forming vast colonies placed where the maximum warmth can be gained from the sun. They are insectivorous, feeding on the many smaller insects and larvae which inhabit the woods.

Above: Wood ant nest
Below: Northern wood ants

Male bullfinch

BIRDS OF THE PENNINE WOODLANDS

Most of the woodlands in the Pennines will support the typical range of woodland or garden birds that you can see almost anywhere in the UK. These include many familiar garden birds like wren, robin, blackbird, song thrush, blue-, great-, coal- and long-tailed tits. The list also includes more typical woodland birds like great-spotted woodpecker, tawny owl, nuthatch, treecreeper, chaffinch and jay. All of these birds are resident so can be seen in Pennine woodlands at any time of year, although the springtime is best, when they will be in full song and the woodland floor is carpeted with colourful flowers.

In addition to these, ash and hazel woodlands also host a characteristic suite of species. Ash trees often develop holes where branches fall, and these are used by redstarts and spotted flycatchers, both of which are summer visitors. The rare and declining marsh tit *(Poecile palustris)* also inhabits damper ash woods in the limestone areas, often announcing its presence with an explosive 'pitchout'.

Green woodpeckers *(Picus viridis)* favour limestone woods where they can dig for ants in the light soils, often excavating a nest in old ash trees whence their loud laughing calls ring out in limestone valleys in the spring.

The seeds from the ash are an important food source for **Bullfinches** *(Pyrrhula pyrrhula)* who nest in the under-storey scrub such as blackthorn or hawthorn. The image above is a male bullfinch.

Warblers

Garden warbler

Warblers are smaller than sparrows and unobtrusive, most of them coloured mid-grey to brown on top, and white to yellow below, so they can be tricky to tell apart. However, their songs are distinctive and, usually, the first sign of their presence. The more common summer migrant warblers found in upland woods include chiffchaffs, garden warblers and blackcaps.

The **Wood Warbler** *(Phylloscopus sibilatrix)* is a trans-Saharan migrant which visits our northern oak woods for the spring and summer months. It is quite common across Europe, but increasingly rare in the UK, favouring mature, open oak woods. It has silky white underparts with a lemon wash on the throat. Wood warblers nest among vegetation on the forest floor but prefer woods without a shrubby understorey. It sings from high in the trees with an alternative call: one is an accelerating trill and the second is a slower ringing pew-pew-pew-pew. It was first defined as a separate species in the UK by Gilbert White, the great eighteenth-century Hampshire naturalist, who noticed that the wood warbler song was different from both the chiffchaff and the willow warbler. He proposed the more descriptive name of 'the large shivering willow wren'.

Chiffchaff

The **Willow Warbler** *(Phylloscopus sibilatrix)* is a common summer migrant which is similar in appearance to the chiffchaff but has more yellow in the plumage and paler legs. Its song is a sweet descending scale that declares to all who hear it that springtime has arrived.

Willow warbler

Wood warbler

Blackcap

Other less common birds

The **Tree Pipit** (*Anthus trivialis*) is a summer migrant which, in spite of its name, spends much of its life on the ground, where it also nests. It likes woodland that is very open, so frequents young conifer plantations or well-spaced oak and birch trees where it may be seen, often singing, perched on the branches. The tree pipit has a very similar appearance to its much more common cousin, the meadow pipit. Tree pipits feed on insects and have a characteristic habit of pumping their tails.

The **Redstart** (*Phoenicurus phoenicurus*) arrives from Africa in April and is then quite widespread in open woodlands, particularly where oak predominates. They nest in holes in trees, but also in hedgerows and old barns, feeding on flying insects and also visiting trees for their larvae. The males are unmistakable, with a grey back and black mask whilst females are much plainer. Their rattling song is a familiar soundtrack to the Pennines in spring. If you are fortunate enough to be able to watch them, redstarts have a habit of quivering or twitching their tails.

Male redstart

Tree pipit

The name redstart means red tail: this is possessed by both males and females, although it is more orange in colour rather than a proper red. The use of 'red' to cover a range of colours at the red end of the spectrum derives from the use of the word before the late eighteenth century when Isaac Newton split white light into its component colours. Originally, the term ' orange' applied to the fruit, but later transferred to the colour.

The **Pied Flycatcher** (*Ficedula hypoleuca*) is another African migrant arriving in our northern oak woods in the spring. It is restricted to upland Britain and prefers mature woods where natural nest cavities can be found, old woodpecker holes being a favourite. However they will readily use nest boxes and in many places their numbers have been bolstered by nest box provision. Males are strikingly black and white, with a glaring white wing patch which is displayed with wing flips like semaphore whereas the females are brown and much plainer.

Pied flycatcher males have a tendency to court more than one female, but individual females raise more chicks when the male is monogamous and can be a better provider of food. As a result, females have evolved to be very choosy, demanding a lengthy courtship before committing to breed. By this means, the males are given less time to court an unpaired second female.

The redpoll has been in a state of taxonomic flux recently. The form that breeds in Britain is known as the lesser redpoll and the Scandinavian form that visits in winter is the common, or mealy redpoll. The two types have now been lumped together so that our British **Lesser Redpoll** is just a race (*cabaret*) of **Common Redpoll** (*Carduelis flammea*).

They are small, streaky, brown finches whose adult males usually display red across the head and breast. Their preferred breeding habitat is birch scrub and new forestry plantations where they feed on alder seeds and birch catkins. In winter they are often found feeding in mixed flocks in larch plantations with siskins.

Pied flycatcher

The name redpoll refers to the red patch on the forehead, as the word 'poll' originally meant head: this is the derivation of the use of the word 'poll' as a vote or head count. It now only survives in its original meaning when describing the part between the ears on a horse or cow, or its use in the term 'poll–axe' which refers to chopping heads rather than trees.

Common redpoll

The **Woodcock** *(Scolopax rusticola)* is a rather sturdy wader, that is attracted to damp, marshy places within wooded areas. It is crepuscular (emerging mostly at dawn and dusk), so although the light may be poor, dusk is the most likely time to actually see woodcock. In daytime they remain very still and quiet, their striped brown plumage providing excellent camouflage. A person may walk within a few feet of a woodcock nest and it will remain absolutely still, invisibility being its selected option for survival. They breed in the UK but are joined by a larger contingent of birds which fly in from Russia and Scandinavia to overwinter.

From April till June, the males fly in a breeding display known as roding, covering a wide area and flying with slow, measured wing-beats over the treeline whilst emitting a low growling sound, interspersed with a high-pitched squeaky sneeze. Where they encounter other males, they compete to attract the attention of females and the opportunity to breed.

Above: Flying woodcock

Below: Woodcock in its nest

BIRDS FOUND IN CONIFEROUS PLANTATIONS

A densely-packed, dark monoculture coniferous forest is not a very friendly place for any creature or plant as they can be very dark and impenetrable at the forest floor level, and the falling needles create acid conditions. Also, although mature conifers produce numerous seeds in the pine cones which can be a valuable source of food for birds, most plantation conifers are felled before they mature, so they provide little food for birds.

However, plantation forests do vary considerably in their structure depending upon the species planted and the level of management. For instance, European larch trees are deciduous, and where they are well-managed and allowed to mature, they result in a more open forest. Also, in a few places, work is being done to thin out conifers and plant broad-leaved species to restore mixed woodland and so create a diverse habitat which is more wildlife-friendly.

Some of the species which can be encountered in coniferous woodland are described below.

Tall larches and Scots pines are favoured as nesting sites for **Goshawks** (*Accipiter gentilis*) and the much smaller **Sparrowhawk** (*Accipiter nisus*), which are most likely to be seen in the Pennines when they make display flights over the woods during March.

The European larch produces relatively small seeds inside its cones, and these are eaten by siskins and redpolls, which also consume the seeds in the catkins of birch and alder trees.

They spend most of their time feeding high in the canopy, so are best seen when they come down to drink, which is often, thanks to the dry nature of their food.

Above: A sparrowhawk consuming a blackbird

Left: Watchful goshawk in mature pine trees

Siskin

The **Siskin** *(Carduelis spinus)* is a small finch with predominantly yellow colouring and a forked tail. It is a permanent resident in the Pennines but one that is worth looking out for in the winter as many more siskins fly into the UK to take advantage of our milder winters. They will also be found taking advantage of bird feeders in gardens.

You are likely to hear the bird that is one of the most numerous in coniferous forests before you see it – as **Goldcrests** *(Regulus regulus)* flutter among the branches, feeding and making their high-pitched, rather squeaky call: the pitch is so high that some people cannot hear them at all. This is Britain's smallest bird and though its plumage is predominately dull grey-green, it has a bright gold or orange strip between black bars over its head. The goldcrest feeds on insects found among the branches and needles of

Goldcrest

coniferous trees. We have a large, resident population in the Pennines and the numbers are augmented in winter by an influx of Scandinavian birds.

The **Crossbill** *(Loxia curvirostra)* is a native bird that occurs in mature Pennine pinewoods but is easily missed. It feeds inconspicuously on pine cones, high up in the canopy, often only betraying its presence by its jip-jip call. Its diet of dry seeds seems to demand frequent drinks so they are perhaps most often seen descending to puddles to drink. It is a solid-looking finch with a bill whose upper and lower mandibles cross over at the tip: the lower mandible can tilt either way, so some birds are left-tilted while others are right-tilted. The crossed-over mandibles facilitate prising apart the hard scales of a cone from any direction to reach the seed within.

The male crossbill is brick red in colour, with dark wings but, in stark contrast, the female is green. They start breeding very early in the year, even in January, and when the chicks hatch they are fed on a porridge of mashed up pine seeds.

Male crossbill breaking open a pine cone

Female crossbill

plantations, but their numbers vary with the cycles in field vole numbers. Hunting birds can be surprisingly difficult to tell from short-eared owls in the twilight.

In a few places where conifer plantations have been felled, the elusive **Nightjar** *(Caprimulgus europaeus)* moves in. This is a nocturnal bird that rarely flies when it is light enough to see and they are very difficult to find on the ground.

You will know if one is flying by its nocturnal 'churring', which sounds like a distant motorbike.

Nightjars resemble kestrels in shape and size, but their flight has a twisting and turning character, and they do not habitually hover as they are hunting moths rather than ground-dwelling voles. They nest in a scrape on the ground, often in a recently-felled plantation.

They are not a common bird in the Pennines, and have a patchy distribution, being more numerous on lowland heaths.

Left: A long-eared owl
Below: Nightjar on its nest
Opposite: Nightjar in flight

The **Long-eared Owl** *(Asio otus)* is a predator of the woodland edges and heaths. They nest inside the forest, but never build a nest themselves, preferring to use old crow nests, and very occasionally will nest on the ground like a short-eared owl. They are largely nocturnal, emerging from the woods around sunset to hunt in vole-rich habitats including grassland or on the moors. They are not uncommon in the Pennines, and often nest in forestry

MAMMALS IN THE PENNINE WOODLANDS

Mammals have not featured prominently in this book so far, apart from the voles and mountain hares, in spite of the fact that mammals have the biggest impact on the Pennines. This is because the activities of humans, dogs, cats, cattle and sheep are brought about by human activity rather than through being part of a natural habitat, which is the focus of this book. Mammals are at the heart of Pennine agriculture and their husbandry has resulted in the landscape looking the way it does, having removed the trees and kept it that way by grazing. In addition, top predators such as wolves and lynxes have been driven out of the Pennines, along with beavers which were perceived to make things untidy.

Humans have also caused the introduction of many non-native invasive species including grey squirrels, American mink and other aggressive foreign species which continue to reduce the numbers of native animals with which they compete.

The remaining wild mammals are those that either were not perceived as a problem for agriculture, or which have managed to adapt to the changing habitat. The absence of top predators has resulted in numbers of deer (native and introduced) remaining healthy, to the point at which herds need to be culled in many places. On the other hand, the presence of a stable population of top predators indicates a healthy wildlife community.

The woodlands probably support considerably more mammals than the other Pennine habitats because there is plenty of cover and no grazing or poisons. Red squirrels and the dormouse are the focus of several projects to restore numbers, following drastic declines. Foxes, badgers, stoats and weasels are the predators while voles, rabbits and mice are the main mammalian prey.

Bats are often seen flying at dusk, but mainly at lower altitudes where there are trees and buildings in which they can roost. They are all insectivorous, and most of them hunt night-flying insects by emitting high-frequency sounds along with a specialised echo-location capability to detect the exact position of prey. They breed in buildings or trees,

A red squirrel

but as winter approaches, some bats travel long distances to hibernate in limestone caves in the Pennines where the temperature is fairly constant.

Specialist equipment is needed to identify individual species of bats, but those found in the region include pipistrelles, long-eared, daubenton's, and natterer's bats.

The only native mammals that are likely to be seen by a daytime visitor are red squirrels, roe deer, and rabbits in the clearings. Wood mice, bank voles, stoats and weasels are also likely to be present, but are seldom actually seen as they will hear or smell a human before they get close, and take cover.

Grey squirrels *(Sciurus carolinensis)* are another American incomer and are found almost everywhere there are trees in the Pennines, along with most of the rest of Britain. However, there are still one or two wild populations of the native **Red Squirrel** *(Sciurus vulgaris)* in the North Pennines which have, so far, avoided being displaced by their American cousins. There is currently a Red Squirrel Trail at Snaizeholme near Hawes that welcomes visitors.

Roe deer photographed in Malham Tarn Moss where there is a discrete roe deer community

Weasels are present throughout the Pennines but not easily spotted

Stoat

Places to Find Limestone Cloughs

The dale in the White Peak district containing the river Wye, which starts at Buxton then flows through Monsal Dale to Bakewell, contains many clough woods, some of which are ancient, as well as limestone outcrops and scree, flower-rich meadows and grazed pastures.

In the Yorkshire Dales, the most extensive area containing limestone woods is Wharfedale. The woodlands occur within a beautiful and varied landscape including scrub, grassland, mire and limestone scar.

Places to Find Oak and Birch Woods

Although Wharfedale is principally a limestone area, Strid Wood near Bolton Abbey is the largest remnant of oak wood in the National Park.

Another oak wood remnant is Yarncliff Wood in Nether Padley in the White Peaks.

Oak and birch cloughs occur in many locations on the Pennine slopes in the Peak District, although most are quite small.

Below: Nan Scar Clough above Leeming in West Yorkshire. This image was taken at 300 metres altitude on the slopes of Oxenhope Moor. The immediate area is used intensively for grazing and water management, and there is a large wind farm at the top (450 metres). The wood is mostly oak and the ground is covered in bilberry in the foreground, but beyond the fence, it is moor grass.

Pennine Woodland SSSIs

SSSI Name	Approx Location	County	Area	O.S.Grid
Upper Wharfedale	Wharfedale	N Yorks	1123	SD 965735
The Wye Valley	Monsal Dale	Derbyshire	593	SK 154722
Abney & Bretton Cloughs	Hathersage	Derbyshire	147.7	SK 210790
Bastow Wood	Grassington	N Yorks	128.6	SD 990657
Clough Woods	Darley Dale	Derbyshire	119	SK 255615
Coombs Dale	Stoney Middleton	Derbyshire	93	SK 224744
Grass Wood	Wharfedale	N Yorks	88	SD 985655
Scoska Wood	Littondale	N Yorks	70	SD 915725
Stoney Middleton	Stoney Middleton Dale south of Eyam	Derbyshire	69	SK 210760
Strid Wood	River Wharfe near Bolton Abbey	N Yorks	59	SE 070560
Topley Pike & Deepdale	Wye Dale east of Buxton	Derbyshire	50	SK 106724
Kisdon Force Woods	East of Keld, Swaledale	N Yorks	38	NY 900009
Yarncliff Wood Padley	Nether Padley, Near Grindleford	Derbyshire	26	SK 255795
Freeholders Wood	Aysgarth, Wensleydale	N Yorks	14	SE 013889
Ling Gill	East of Ribblehead	N Yorks	5	SD 801785

The river Twiss at Thornton Force near Ingleton

CHAPTER SIX

Aquatic Habitats

Up to 5 metres (200 inches) of rain falls on the Pennine Hills each year with the wettest areas being in the north and west of the range. Moisture-laden clouds blow in on the prevailing Atlantic winds and, as the land rises, the water they contain falls as rain. Where it falls on blanket bog, the water is absorbed by sphagnum moss, or sinks into the peat to be released gradually, but on the heaths and grasslands there is little to stop it running off downhill into the many streams and rivers. This water sustains the bogs and heaths and, over millennia, it shapes the landscape, weathering

steep-sided dales and cutting into the limestone to form caves and crags.

The rounded peaks of the Pennines form an east-west watershed from which water drains into becks that join rivers which either flow east, like the Don, Calder, Wharfe and Ure, across the plains of Yorkshire to the North Sea, or else they take the shorter westerly route through Lancashire to the Irish Sea and these rivers include the Ribble and Eden. In many cases, the flow is interrupted by the dozens of dams situated across the entire Pennine range whose

Stainforth Force on the river Ribble

reservoir waters supply the towns and cities on either side. Although there are times when people long for the rain to stop and the sun to break through, both human enterprise and wildlife survival in the region depend upon it. We were reminded of what a precious resource water is when, in 2018, it took only a couple of months of dry weather for the reservoirs to become severely depleted, causing alarm and restrictions on water consumption. Unfortunately the moors became so desiccated that they were prone to being set alight by carelessness or vandalism and burned for many days in several areas.

As we shall see, along the Pennines there is a wide range of aquatic habitats from bog pools to lakes and reservoirs, and from small fast-flowing streams in a variety of conditions to rivers which can be characterised by rapids and waterfalls, or else wide and slow-flowing. The impact of man is seen in the canals and also in the rivers that are channelled and controlled by weirs, dams and sluices. Historically, the waterways have been radically altered to serve the needs of mine-workings, quarries and mills, most of which are now defunct, but whose structures remain, channelling their flow.

High up on the moors, the nature of the water in the many becks which drain the Pennines defines the natural community which they support, and that depends on their source: those originating from blanket bogs on millstone grit are very acidic and contain very little calcium whilst those emanating from the carboniferous limestone are

The river Wharfe after a dry spell, showing the eroded limestone river bed which is coated in algae. The dale side is grazed, and populated by hawthorn trees.

usually saturated with calcium carbonate and so are mildly alkaline (pH >7). The absence of calcium and other mineral ions in acidic water restricts which plants can grow and also makes it difficult for invertebrates such as snails to form their shells. The presence or absence of species of algae, water plants and small invertebrates defines which larger species will be able to thrive and so, to an extent, they determine the ecology of the entire Pennine range.

Most becks and smaller rivers in the uplands are shallow and descend steeply, so the water is very turbulent, preventing sediment from gathering on their rocky beds.

However algae can colonise the rocky surfaces under the water, while liverworts and mosses often do well on the damp surfaces above the stream. These simple plants provide food and habitat for small aquatic animals, such as shrimps and insect larvae, which need to be robust enough to cope with extreme changes in the level of water as the rainfall comes and goes.

A gill tumbling down from the high fells above Langstrothdale

On their way down from the heights, the Pennine becks and small rivers cascade over a number of spectacular waterfalls, such as Hardraw Force and Thornton Force in the Dales; and Ashgill-, High- and Low-Force in the North Pennines. These, along with the spectacular erosion of river beds are a great feature of Pennine limestone areas, and one that is ever-changing as the water rushes down the steep inclines, scooping out hollows, channels and caverns.

The numerous waterfalls and rapids ensure that the water is well-oxygenated, but the speed of the current prevents sediments from accumulating, so that any aquatic creatures, such as nymphs of mayflies and stoneflies, have to be specialists. They need to be streamlined and able to grip the rocks and algae in order not to be carried away by the current.

Caddisfly and stonefly larvae here commonly have large hooks on their rear to enable them to hang on and the protective case is replaced by a silken web attached to a rock.

An odder feature of the streams in the limestone areas is that there are places where becks and quite large rivers disappear, leaving a dry river bed or, in some cases, the river falls through a crack into the caverns below, only to re-emerge into daylight somewhere else lower down and often some distance away. For instance, the beck that drains Malham Tarn disappears underground less than a kilometre from its origin, and Fell Beck on Ingleborough falls down a hole to drop 100 metres down to the floor of Gaping Gill Cave. From there it flows through the extensive cave system before emerging and joining the river Ribble.

Such streams are important as they carry organisms and sediments from the surface into the underground environment enabling the colonisation of these dark places.

Pennine streams arise quite suddenly from springs and underground rivers. One example occurs in the image opposite, where the river Ribble high up its dale, just below Ribblehead, suddenly turns from a rushing beck to a much wider river when the overground stream is joined by one emerging from under the limestone cliff.

This place is also of interest because its sand and gravel bed are important for fish reproduction, providing suitable conditions for salmon and brown trout to spawn. The calmer water allows aquatic plants to grow which provide food, shelter and anchorage points for smaller invertebrates, snails and fish. However, algae and other plants attached to rocks in these waters need to be able to withstand drying out when the water level drops, yet be sufficiently robust to cope when the river is in spate.

As rivers mature, they slow and deepen and more silt collects, added to by falling leaves and other detritus. In well-oxygenated, non-acidic waters, the presence of trees is often a positive for aquatic life, as the decomposition of organic material such as fallen leaves, supports bacteria on which micro-organisms feed and provides nutrients

Headwaters of the river Ribble, where it broadens and shows a gravelly bed

for algae. These tiny organisms, along with the organic detritus in which they thrive, form the bottom of the food chain, sustaining the worms, insects, crustaceans, molluscs and vertebrates which feed on them.

However, the species composition of any stream is entirely dependent on the quality of the water in it, and is compromised by changes in acidity, nutrient content (nitrates, phosphates and ammonium), pesticides and turbidity. Pollution by acid rain, nutrient-rich run-off from agricultural land or from human waste will change the species make-up and fundamentally undermine the ecology. In the higher uplands, there is a low level of human development, so the potential for pollution is low, although waterways are susceptible to acid rain, which results from industrial atmospheric pollution. There are also some disused mine-workings which release metal and other residues into surrounding water.

The likelihood of pollution increases with decreasing altitude because as farming intensifies, settlements become larger and the number of inputs from industry and sewage systems grow.

NATURAL LAKES AND SMALLER WATERBODIES

Only two natural lakes of any size exist along the length of the Pennines, both in the Yorkshire Dales. This is because the Pennine chain has no deep, closed valleys and also because the limestone that is the bedrock over much of the area is too porous and faulted for water to collect on the surface to form ponds or lakes.

The largest natural lake is Malham Tarn, which only extends to 60 hectares and with a maximum depth of just over four metres. It sits on a ledge of impermeable silurian slate, covered with thick deposits of marl and clay. Because most of the streams that feed it flow across limestone, the water is slightly alkaline (pH 8.25 average) which makes it a unique waterbody in Britain.

The second lake is Semer Water in Raydale, off Wensleydale, which extends to over 31 hectares, but has an average depth of less than one metre. Semer Water is the remains of a much larger waterbody that was trapped by moraine at the end of an Ice Age glacier. It was never very deep, but has become increasingly shallow mainly due to large quantities of sediment collecting in it.

In addition to these lakes there are some hundreds of small tarns, almost all among the bogs and moors where gritstone is the bedrock. The water in these tends to be strongly acidic and this, combined with the harsh conditions, means that these tarns support limited animal and plant life, although what survives there is specialist and can be intriguing.

There is also a number of small dams and ponds associated with the historic lead mining industry, many of which contain high concentrations of lead and other metal ions. Although they have remained undisturbed for a hundred years or more, some of these workings still release

Semer Water, after a period of low rainfall

Old Pennine lead mine workings near Pately Bridge in the Yorkshire Dales

metal ions into the surrounding flushes, mires and streams resulting in changes in local plant communities.

Attitudes to pollution have changed dramatically since these mines were working back in the nineteenth century, when the poisonous emissions from the works could pollute not only the water, but the surrounding land. Entire plant communities were destroyed, leaving bare rock and earth behind. In most cases, these have still not recovered, but the metal-tolerant plant communities which have taken over the spoil-heaps and metal-containing flushes are now protected in their own right because of

interest in the unusual flora occurring there.

In this chapter, we will explore the flora and fauna of small tarns and becks high up on the moors, then look at the two natural lakes before following the waterways down as they broaden into rivers. Aquatic habitats in the Pennines are very diverse, so this book will be far from comprehensive in its coverage, but will hopefully provide some broad insights into these habitats.

WILDLIFE IN THE PENNINE WATERWAYS

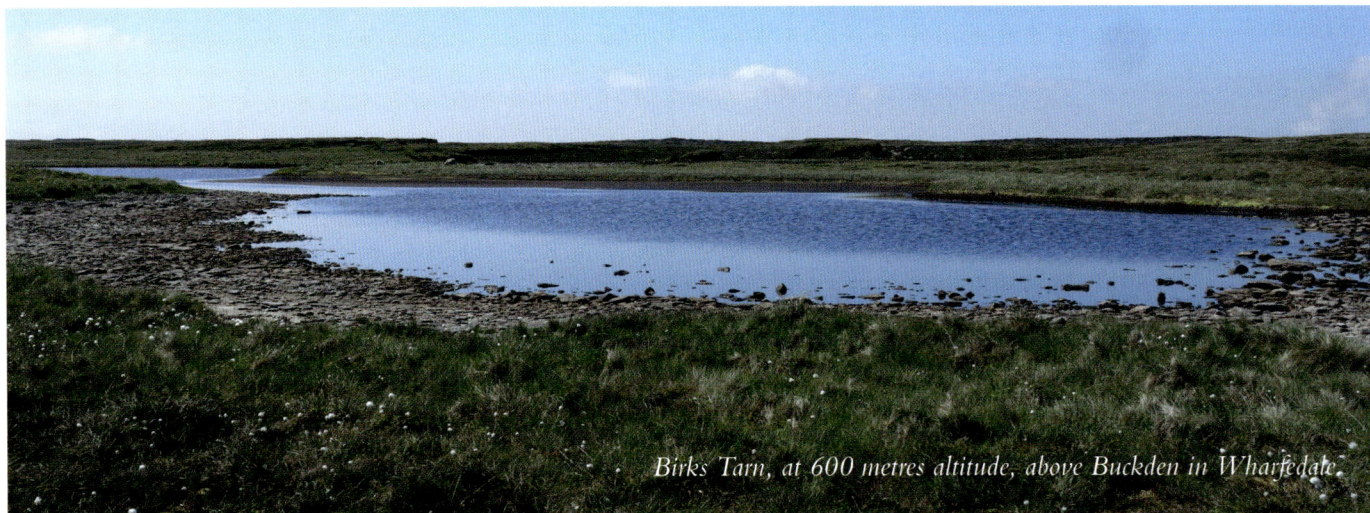

Birks Tarn, at 600 metres altitude, above Buckden in Wharfedale.

UPLAND TARNS AND BECKS

Malham Tarn and Semer Water are referred to as 'lakes' in this text, because they are the largest natural waterbodies in the Pennines: there is no standard for describing a stretch of water as a 'pool', 'pond', 'tarn' or 'lake'. Nor does any standard define when a 'rill' or 'gill' becomes a 'beck', or 'stream' becomes a river. In this section we are discussing the smaller pools, tarns and head-water streams.

Almost all the natural tarns in the Pennines are situated in the millstone grit areas where peat predominates and the ground water, which feeds the tarns, is acidic. Studies at Fountains Fell Tarn [Gilbert et al., Field Studies Council] and others consistently reveal a pH of around 4 (highly acidic) and extremely low concentrations of calcium and other ions. Few species of algae or bryophytes can cope with the harsh conditions in and around the edges of such pools, especially when the acidity is aggravated by extreme changes in pool depth, to the point of drying out in hot weather.

The Fountains Fell study reports heavily-leached flat pieces of gritstone, similar to those comprising the floor of Birks Tarn (right), supporting only a tiny quantity of Porpidia lichens and no algae. In such places, aquatic plants and phytoplankton cannot get established so there is little food for aquatic animals. The image of the bed of Birks Tarn follows a dry period (so the water was low) in which the water is stained with peat, and the rocks and bottom remain clear of readily recognisable algal growth. (There are algae that will grow on rock surfaces in low nutrient, acidic conditions which can be a component of the brownish slime of the tarn bed.)

The gills that start in the peat bogs are similarly challenging to life but, according to the same study, can support quite a range of algae, bryophytes and lichens. They may be relatively clear of obvious pond life in the winter, when the flows are highest, but with the spring, red and green algae and diatoms multiply, especially if mosses and liverwort mats are present. With summer, the flow in

Above: A moss with sporangia on Birks Moor

Below left: A pool containing green algae

streams often reduces and may cease altogether, and the bed may become a great mat of algae or mosses. The image on the left is of a puddle on a typical blanket bog in summer which contains a growth of matted green alga.

Bryophytes do well at the water's edge in the grit-stone bogs: not only sphagnum, but other mosses and liverworts can become quite large, providing a fertile habitat for diatoms and other phytoplankton as well as zooplankton.

A few aquatic crustacean species, such as the freshwater shrimp *(Gammarus pulex)*, do occur in small blanket bog pools but they have great difficulty in forming a shell because of the acidity, so they are insufficient in numbers to support larger organisms. However, some creatures are adapted to live on, rather than in the water, so avoiding the acidity, such as the insects overleaf on the surface of a blanket bog pool.

The **Common Pond Skater** *(Gerris lacustris)* is one of the most widespread British bugs, which can be found on many waterbodies, including this little pool in Tarn Moss. They are true bugs (the Hemiptera order of insects) and carnivorous, preying on smaller invertebrates, for which the pair of forelegs is adapted. These are folded up beneath the insect's head, whilst the two remaining pairs of legs enable it to treat the water surface as its highway.

There are other, more specialist high altitude, acid-loving species of water boatman, notably *Arctocorisa carinata* found on these pools.

The water cricket (see page 30) is another bug inhabiting the surface of ponds, which has some interesting behaviour giving it an advantage in this challenging habitat. It is distasteful to most predators, such as fish, and can speed its travel across the water surface by squirting detergent-like saliva onto it which reduces the surface tension.

The small rills and becks flowing across the high peaty moors remain challenging for aquatic life owing to the acidity, but this situation changes where the water meets the limestone.

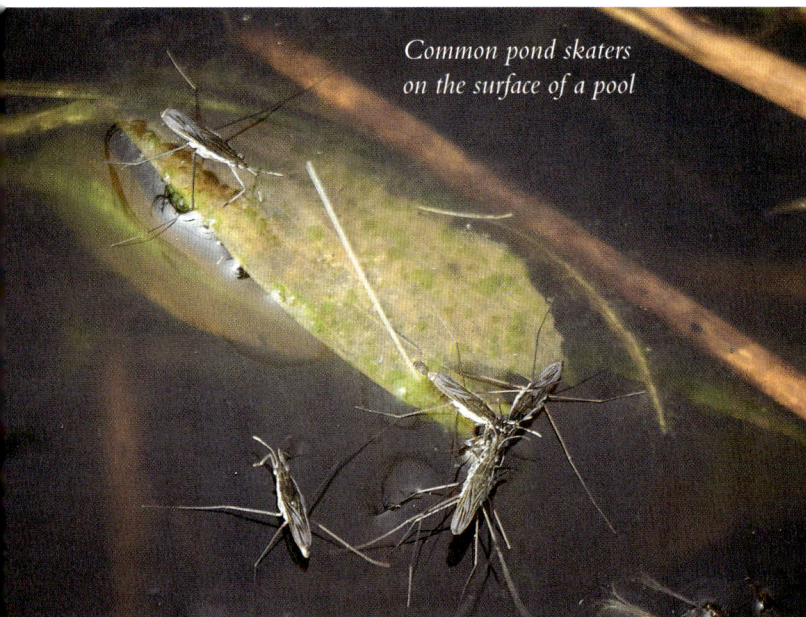

Common pond skaters on the surface of a pool

Invertebrates of the limestone pools and streams

The few pools, along with the many flushes and streams that occur on limestone, are often far richer in aquatic life as the water emanating from limestone springs has a pH of at least 7 and contains quite high concentrations of calcium and other minerals. Flushes – damp, flat areas with a small pool or mire – often surround such springs where algae can thrive along with aquatic plants such as spiked water milfoil *(Myriophyllum spicatum)*, supporting aquatic snails, crustaceans and insect larvae in the water while mosses and liverworts cover the surrounding ground.

Freshwater shrimp

Freshwater shrimps such as *Gammarus pulex*, can occur in large numbers in the less acidic, quieter waters of the Pennines. They are 'amphipod' crustaceans which feed on organic detritus in the water and are very important in consuming organic material in waterways, so assisting in preventing them silting up. They are also an important food source for larger creatures.

Many insects, including dragonfly, mayfly, stonefly, caddisfly and midges, have aquatic larval stages which dwell in the mud and under stones in ponds and streams. These larvae may remain growing in the mud for years, taking up most of the life-span of the species and representing an important component of the aquatic community of species.

Caddisflies, or 'sedge flies' can be mistaken for moths as adults, but their larvae live underwater, where most species make protective cases by spinning

Caddisfly larvae

stones, sand, leaves and twigs together with a silk they secrete from glands around the mouth. These cases may be fixed to stones or transportable, although a few species are free-swimming and only construct shelters when they're ready to pupate. One of these is shown in the photograph, crawling on the underside of a bit of limestone picked out of a beck in Wharfedale.

Beneath another stone in the same beck, along with some small snails and larvae, the author noticed a large number of soft, dark-brown flatworms. These are planaria, which are a very simple type of non-parasitic flatworm which live in clean freshwater habitats. Surprisingly, being so soft and small, they predate on aquatic snails and in some places have been found to assist in controlling invasive snail species. They are also special in that they will regenerate complete bodies after being cut into pieces.

The river Twiss tumbling down its course above Ingleton

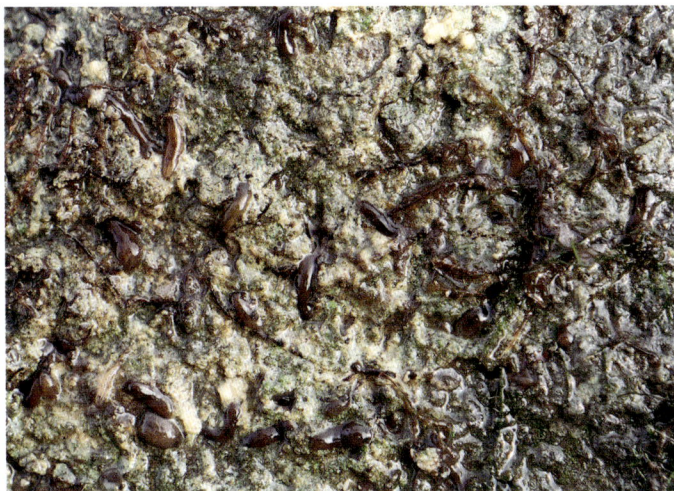

Planarium worms on a rock

Other species found in these limestone waters include water beetles such as *Agabus sp.* and *Oreodytes sp.* and molluscs, such as calcium-loving *Vertigo* species.

Where the land is sloping or steep, the streams that emerge from the springs tend to be shallow and turbulent. Sediment and organic detritus are washed away and the stream beds are usually rocky so that resident organisms tend to be confined to the margins or sheltered places beneath boulders. Even the larger upland Pennine streams are subject to great and rapid variations in their depth as drought follows drenching and both create challenges for resident organisms.

In these smaller streams and rivers, insect larvae remain common as rocks provide shelter, and many are well adapted to coping with varying water levels descending into the gravel in the stream bed to join the burrowing worms and resistant eggs as the water level drops. Again, aquatic shrimps can be common along with two types of mollusc, the wandering snail *(Radix peregra)* and the river limpets *(Ancylus fluviatilis)*: these seem well adapted to the conditions, although they are widespread generalists rather than upland specialists.

Along the stream edges, bryophytes can form mats and cushions, providing shelter for many invertebrate animals and also opportunities for ferns and herbs to take root.

Above: Mosses and a polypody ferns take root on a fallen bough by the river Wye
Below: Mosses and liverworts coat the banks of the river Wharfe at Bolton Abbey

Dipper on a mossy rock

Upland Pennine streams provide habitat for native crayfish and fish, including bullheads, stone loach, grayling and brown trout. The small fish attract predators, so dippers patrol the rocks and kingfishers *(Alcedo atthis)* watch for prey, usually perched on branches above the river.

The **Dipper** *(Cinclus cinclus)* can usually be seen standing on rocks in mid-stream and, although its habits suggest it could be a wader, it isn't one: in fact, it behaves rather like a sandpiper although it is a songbird related to thrushes. However it is superbly adapted to its habitat and is the only British bird that can walk underwater, which they do as they browse for aquatic shrimps, insect larvae and small fish, using their wings to help maintain position.

Dippers have dark plumage with a white throat and have the habit of bobbing up and down. They have a rather complex, subdued song which can be heard in the springtime, although it is often drowned out by the noise of the rushing water. They build dome-shaped nests out of twigs and moss which can be attached to the river bank, rocks or the underside of a bridge.

The **Grey Wagtail** *(Motacilla cinerea)* is another bird that feeds on aquatic insects in fast-flowing streams. Their upper parts are slate grey but their plumage is bright lemon yellow underneath with a tail that is somewhat longer than that of pied and yellow wagtails. They are an upland bird which lives in many countries but are sadly on the Species Red List in the UK, their population having declined at the time of writing by over 50% since 2002.

Grey wagtail

FISH

If the gradient eases so that sand and gravel can accumulate in the stream bed, but the flow is sufficiently strong to prevent the build-up of silt, conditions are suitable for salmon and trout to breed, in which case the flow can be called a 'riffle'.

Salmonids lay their eggs in the late autumn and winter, creating a shallow depression using their tails in the gravelly stream bed, called a 'redd'. For this to happen, it is essential that the water is clear and good quality, and the stream bed is silt-free and undisturbed during spawning.

Once the female has laid her eggs, they are immediately fertilised by the male, who covers them in 'milt' which contains the sperm. The female then covers the eggs in gravel to prevent them being eaten or washed away.

In the spring, the eggs hatch into tiny 'alevins' which still have the yolk sac which is their early food source. As that gets used up, they emerge from the gravel as small 'fry' and start feeding on invertebrates and plankton. It takes several years for them to attain adult size, although the proportion that reach maturity is possibly one per cent.

River Wye near its confluence with the Derwent

A small bullhead, freshwater shrimps and mayfly larvae scooped up while monitoring invertebrates in a Pennine stream bed

In the gravel of the upper river Eden, lampreys lay their eggs alongside the Atlantic salmon and brown trout in riffles. Two of the three British species (*Petromyzon marinus* and *Lampetra fluviatilis*) spend part of their lives at sea while the **Brook Lamprey** *(Lampetra planeri)* is freshwater only. Lampreys are fish with a long ancestry that parasitise other fish, such as salmon and trout, by clamping onto them with their mouths which are full of rasping teeth. They were once common in the Yorkshire Dales but are quite rare now, possibly because the numbers of fish to parasitise has decreased along with changes to water quality.

Two other fish are worth mentioning here as they play an important role in the upland river ecosystem. Bullheads (*Cottus gobio*) feed on crustaceans in the becks and small rivers where they hide underneath stones. They are common throughout England, growing up to only about 12cm in length. They have a large head with eyes towards the top and fan-like fins.

The stone loach (*Barbatula barbatula*) is a small slender fish which lives amongst the gravel and stones of fast-flowing water where it can feel for crustaceans and other invertebrate prey species with the fleshy 'barbels' around its mouth.

of the image opposite. It is a native species, but one which has become an invasive pest in the United States because it spreads by producing lots of seed and also by growing from fragments. Once established it can produce thick mats which overcome other aquatic plants and block waterways.

Along with the many mosses and liverworts, common reeds and sedges grow along the banks. The common spike-rush *(Eleocharis palustris)* is frequently found, along with some rarities, such as the flowering rush *(Butomus umbellatus)*.

Left: Brook lamprey

Below: Water starwort

AQUATIC PLANTS

In calmer waters where pools are present, silt builds up that contains nutrients and organic debris, enabling rich colonies of micro-organisms and other small invertebrates to thrive. This is particularly the case where trees line the stream as falling leaves and other debris enrich the stream where it collects. Here, aquatic algae, including the stonewort *(Chara vulgaris)* are to be found along with aquatic angiosperms such as broad-leaved pondweed *(Potamogeton natans)* and red pondweed *(Potamogeton alpines)*. **Common water-starwort** *(Callitriche stagnalis)*, as the Latin name suggests, favours pools where the water is slow-flowing or still. The plant in the photograph was at the edge of the River Wye in Derbyshire, at the location

Malham Tarn in winter from the Great Close Hill in the east

WILDLIFE IN THE LAKES, OR BIG TARNS

Malham Tarn is the aquatic jewel of the Pennines, supporting a diverse flora, six species of fish and 24 species of crustacean including the rare white-clawed crayfish. It is 60 hectares in area with an average depth of 2.4 metres and is highly unusual, being in the middle of an area of fractured carboniferous limestone. Water has accumulated here because its bed is made up of several metres of marl (clay sediments and calcium carbonate) laid down on a bedrock of silurian shale since the last Ice Age. The water is mildly alkaline (pH 8.25) because the main inflows derive from limestone springs which arise in places where groundwater in the limestone meets the shale which underlies the Tarn. Although limestone looks like solid rock, water flows within the many fractures and crevices with which it is riddled, as well as in underground streams. At Malham Tarn, this underground water encounters the impervious shale intrusion and has nowhere to go but upwards, until it emerges as a series of springs.

The largest single surface inflow is from a beck that rises in the surrounding grasslands to the west then meanders through the fen which lies along the Tarn's edge,

known as Tarn Moss. On the north shore sits Malham Tarn House which is now owned by the National Trust but is run as the Field Studies Council Field Centre, Malham Tarn. To the east are Great Close Hill and, at its foot, Great Close Mire and Ha Mire, which are boggy areas both crossed by the Pennine Way walking trail.

Water flows out from the lake towards the south in Malham Tarn Beck, which only exists for around half a kilometre before it meets a gap in its limestone bed down which the water falls into the underground cave system. Where this water emerges once more is a mystery as it is not in Malham Beck, which suddenly appears from the base of the Malham Cove cliffs only 1.6 kilometres away. So it seems that streams cross each other at different levels inside the cave system lying behind the cliff. This provides a challenge for cavers who continue to explore the Malham system in an effort to solve the mystery of where the water goes on its journey.

Being so rare and biologically rich, the Tarn and its surroundings are monitored and studied scientifically while the Field Centre is very busy providing accommodation and facilities for educational visitors. The lake is classed as mesotrophic, which is the status between oligotrophic (low in nutrients) and eutrophic (high in nutrients). The water of Malham Tarn has a nutrient content which supports a rich range of localised plant and animal life, but should not allow algal blooms for more than two weeks per year. As it is a shallow lake, it is very vulnerable to extended dry periods when nutrients might become more concentrated or lack oxygen. Constant vigilance and work are required to protect the lake from an increase in nitrate and phosphate concentrations from agricultural run-off as these would jeopardise the habitat and its natural communities.

Malham Tarn, particularly at its margins, is very rich in green algae and mosses and liverworts. A third of its bottom is covered by a deep sward of the **Fragile Stonewort** (*Chara globularis*). Stoneworts are so called because they accumulate encrustations of calcium carbonate, and as the material dies and falls to the bottom, it adds to the marl lake lining. The lake hosts many other species of green alga and waterweed which provide habitats for many small creatures including thirteen species of water snails and nine bivalve molluscs along with shrimps, copepods, flatworms and seven species of leech. Copepods are very small crustaceans which swim about in the water, often in great numbers and two species of these crustaceans, *Bryocamptus rhaeticus* and *Moraria mrazeki*, are

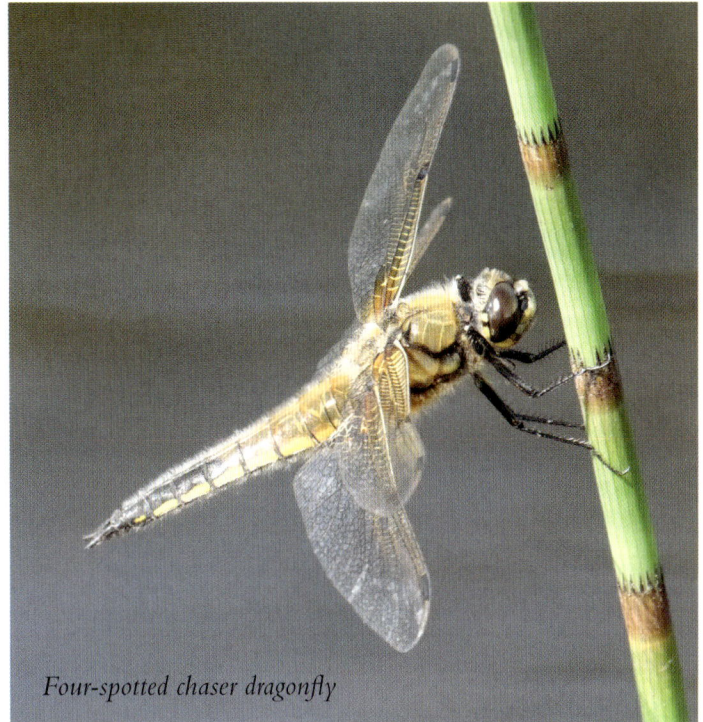

Four-spotted chaser dragonfly

interesting because they are probably relics from the Ice Age: they occur nowhere else in England.

The Tarn, along with its surroundings, is a hot-spot for molluscs, with 62 species of land snails and 25 species of freshwater snails, which probably reflects the great range of habitats that exist within the area. It also supports huge numbers of midge, mayfly, stonefly and caddisfly, the larvae and adults of which are an important food source for both fish and birds. There are many dragonfly species: the **Four-spotted Chaser dragonfly** (*Libellula quadrimaculata*) pictured was one of several present along the beck that flows through Tarn Moss in June, along with azure and large red damselflies. Clouds of (mostly) non-biting midges emerge from the lake in late May whose larvae are a food source for fish and whose emerging adults are a bumper harvest for wagtails, swifts and swallows.

Fragile stonewort (Chara globularis)

White-clawed crayfish

Signal crayfish

The **White-clawed Crayfish** *(Austropotamobius pallipes)* was once common throughout Europe and the UK but its range has reduced dramatically to the point where it remains in a number of isolated strongholds. There are several of these in the Pennines, in particular Malham Tarn and the streams that feed it, where numbers have varied over the years for reasons that are not always clear, but they have a better chance than in most places as the Tarn is not connected directly to any larger waterway (owing to the outflow disappearing into a large cave system).

In the Yorkshire Dales, the white-clawed crayfish is also found in parts of the rivers Wharfe and Ure, often alongside the rival invasive signal crayfish. In the Derbyshire Peak District there may be some in Lathkill Dale, but a recent survey of the Dove/Manifold rivers system found no crayfish whatsoever, although good habitat exists in some places. Occasional isolated populations of native crayfish do occur outside the Pennines, the closest of which may be on the Markeaton Brook within the Derby city boundaries.

The white-clawed crayfish is olive-green to brown in colour and gets its name from the whitish colouration on the undersides of the claws. They come out at night to feed on a broad diet including organic detritus, smaller invertebrates and plant matter.

The main reasons for their decline are the arrival of the larger **American Signal Crayfish** *(Pacificastus leniusculus)* which is more aggressive, depriving the natives of food, along with the crayfish plague fungus that is lethal to the native and carried by the invader. There are projects to reintroduce white-clawed crayfish to certain Pennine waterways, but protecting them from the signal crayfish and the plague so that the introduced populations get established is challenging.

The signal crayfish causes wider problems in British rivers as it breeds very successfully and feeds voraciously on a wide range of organisms, depleting the diets of fish. It also undermines banks with its burrows and they have become so numerous that businesses have been created to trap them and supply their meat to restaurants on some English rivers. However, a licence is required to trap either species of crayfish and it is illegal to transfer signal crayfish from one waterway to another, for which fines can be very heavy.

The wealth of invertebrates in Malham Tarn provides plenty of food for the resident brown trout and perch *(Perca fluviatilis)* as well as the smaller fish including three-spined stickleback *(Gasterosteus aculeatus)*, stone loach and bullhead.

Wading and aquatic birds which breed and use this mosaic of habitats include the coot (*Fulica atra*), snipe, redshank *(Tringa tetanus)*, curlew, common sandpiper *(Actitis hypoleucos)*, lapwing and oystercatcher *(Haematopus ostralegus)*. Canada geese are frequent but unwelcome visitors being both an introduced species and aggressive to other birds.

A few Eurasian otters *(Lutra lutra)* live in the area, feeding mainly on the smaller trout and bullheads: it was a relief to researchers that they do not seem to favour the white-clawed crayfish as it is already under such threat.

More than 100 water voles were reintroduced to Malham Tarn in 2016 and are reported to be thriving and spreading along the surrounding becks. This suggests that the American mink, which infest many English rivers and displace water voles, are not present.

Above: Wigeon were first recorded breeding in the Yorkshire Dales in 1955 and a small number of pairs continue to breed on the upland tarns and reservoirs.

Below: Redshank. These waders are most associated with lowland saltmarshes and estuaries, but in summer months they will seek out inland lakes like Malham Tarn.

*View across Tarn Moss
showing the raised peat bog*

TARN MOSS

In stark contrast to the lake whose west shore it borders, Tarn Moss is a raised peat bog which is acidic, although conditions vary across its breadth as parts of it have been modified by human activity including draining, grazing and peat cutting. The Moss adjoins an area of fen and woodland on its north-west edge which has a quite separate ecology, although the two are often lumped together. The botany of Tarn Moss is typical of that found in the blanket bogs and wet upland heaths, representing another contrast, this time to the surrounding limestone grasslands. Tarn Moss vegetation is sphagnum mosses, common heather, cotton grasses and bog grasses along with crowberry,

bilberry, cowberry, cloudberry and bog rosemary. Bog asphodel and round-leaved sundew are found in the wet places along with several sedge species and abundant leafy liverworts and mosses which form floating mats on many of the pools. Many wetland flowering species occur across the whole area, including marsh cinquefoil (*Comorum palustre*), marsh marigold, marsh bedstraw (*Galium palustre*) and ragged robin (*Lychnis flos-cuculi*).

The photograph above is taken from the boardwalk across the fen looking south over Tarn Moss, which is the raised, duller green area in the middle of the picture. Continuous growth and deposition of sphagnum mosses has resulted in the bog rising above the tarn and the adjacent fen, which is in the foreground of the photograph where cotton grasses and alder are dominant. The wood in the distance is Spiggot Hill which lies within the Moss at the western edge of the Tarn.

In addition to the Tarn itself and its varied shoreline, twelve National Vegetation Classification (NVC) communities occur within the area, from sphagnum pools and molinia mires, to sedge mires, willow and birch woodland to grass pasture.

The Fen contains several of these habitats within its modest area which the public can access on the boardwalk through the Fen. From this vantage point, the visitor can get a feel for the character of each habitat as well as potentially seeing a huge range of organisms from the many flowering plants, to pond life, birds and the possibility of sighting of water voles, otters and deer. This is a really special walk at any time of year for anyone interested in nature and it is quite easily accessed by road or footpath from anywhere within the Wharfedale-Ribblesdale area.

The nature and extent of the surroundings of Malham Tarn have changed over the centuries as landowners have, at times, attempted to increase the amount of grazing land through drainage and soil improvement measures.

Agricultural activities have ceased since the National Trust took over, but pressures continue both from pollution by the nutrients in ground water and from visitor numbers. Even studying the habitats can bring its own problems through disturbance of wildlife or physical damage to the land. It is important that people understand what is present and how the ecosystem works as ignorance often lies behind far more significant damage.

This placid lake is indeed a very special and important natural feature of the Dales and of Great Britain. It is easily enjoyed in passing by the many Pennine Way hikers and motorists, but investing a little time on its shores, or the boardwalk, will be well rewarded.

Bogbean

Globeflower

Ragged robin

View of Semer Water

SEMER WATER

Semer Water (also known as Lake Semerwater) sits in Raydale, which is a small, rather pretty offshoot of Wensleydale, due north of the top end of Wharfedale. Raydale is an island of fairly level land surrounded by high moors, so it is farmed mostly for sheep. The green pasture is relieved by an attractive scattering of deciduous woodland among the fields and on the dale sides. Semer Water is about half the size of Malham Tarn but less than a metre deep, the water sitting on many metres of sediment that is mostly brought in by Crooks Beck from the high bogs to the south, but also from agricultural activities. Like Malham Tarn, it is mesotrophic (ie neither high nor low in nutrients), but that status is even more fragile than in Malham Tarn owing to its lack of depth and the proximity of actively managed farmland.

Whilst Malham Tarn has not suffered unduly from government-inspired agricultural initiatives, there were attempts to drain Semer Water and its surrounding marshes in 1937. This may have been inspired by the need to grow more food in wartime when cargo ships were being targeted by U-boats. More recently, work has been done to persuade the local farmers to engage in environmental stewardship schemes which provide grants for protecting waterbodies from nutrient-rich run-off from the land. In spite of this, the water is of indifferent quality and the lake is colonised by the introduced Canadian pondweed *(Elodea Canadensis)* and Nuttall's pondweed *(Elodea nuttallii)*. However it supports a large number of mayfly species and a population of white-clawed crayfish along with many other smaller crustacean species which feed good numbers of brown trout, perch and roach, making it a popular destination for anglers.

Around the lake margins there are swamps containing common club-rush *(Schoenoplectus lacustris)*, several sedges, bogbean and a swathe of yellow water-lily *(Nuphar lutea)* which produces a brilliant display of colour in July. There is a stretch of carr woodland along the western shoreline, comprised of alder and willow species.

Beyond the lake shores and margins, the land is almost all improved pasture apart from the very highest points which turn to heath.

RESERVOIRS

There are a lot of reservoirs across the Pennine Hills: Yorkshire Water manages dozens of them, along with Severn Trent and two other companies. They range in size from Ladybower, which is four kilometres long and covers an area of 210 hectares, to small installations like Ryburn, in the Yorkshire Dales, at only 10 hectares. Most have been created by taking advantage of the shape of the land and simply building a dam across river valleys and leaving them to fill up. The towns and cities below rely entirely on the reservoirs for the provision of clean water, and this responsibility is taken so seriously that water companies have ownership of large stretches of land across their catchments where development and disturbance of the land are kept to a minimum. This has protected expanses of moorland and also created beautiful landscape features, albeit at the cost of the land, wildlife and communities that were drowned.

The water in higher reservoirs tends to be very low in nutrients (oligotrophic) because they are fed mostly by acidic water from the bogs, and there are no trees dropping leaves nor fertiliser run-off from farms. Therefore biodiversity in and around high reservoirs tends to be quite limited compared to the natural lakes, such as Malham Tarn. The sort of bird species likely to be encountered in the high reservoirs are mallard ducks and common sandpipers, along with Canada geese and visits from normally marine birds such as gulls and oystercatchers.

Many of the lower reservoirs do support a wider range of fish and other wildlife and angling is permitted to

Bradfield Dale and Strines Reservoir

the extent that some of them are artificially stocked with trout and the fishing rights sold.

The photograph above is looking over Bradfield Dale in south Yorkshire which contains the Strines Reservoir. There is a semi-natural oak clough wood in the foreground, and coniferous forest plantations spread across the dale side in the distance. Plantations were frequently placed adjacent to reservoirs and are managed commercially, but these days, leisure activities including rambling, riding and cycling are encouraged where land is owned by the Forestry Commission and other public bodies. Many of the species described in the Woodlands chapter can be found in these woods, especially where management is less intensive.

As in many other locations, the moorland that rises above the reservoir is maintained for grouse shooting so shooting butts and access tracks have been constructed. Predators are discouraged, disease control is deployed, and tracks and butts are installed for the annual shoots. Derwent Edge, which rises from here, and Bradfield Dale, contain little in the way of houses and agriculture, and the area is close to Sheffield, which makes it quite unusual, and an area which could be a natural resource for local urban dwellers if it were to be re-wilded.

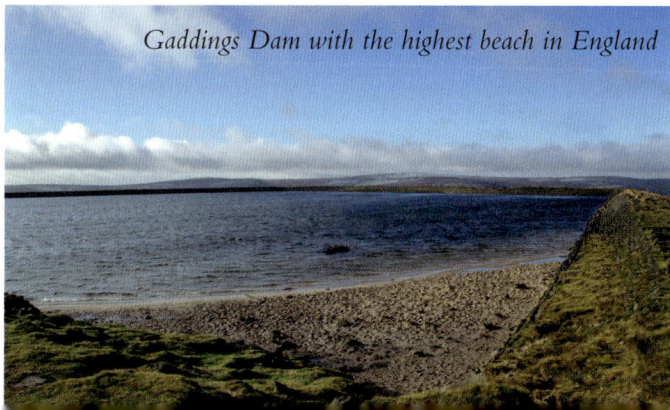
Gaddings Dam with the highest beach in England

Left: One of the ponds that is part of the industrial remains above Hebden Bridge

HERITAGE INDUSTRY AND WATERWAYS

The Industrial Revolution would not have thrived as it did, on both sides of the Pennine Hills, had there not been a plentiful supply of water and many rivers flowing off them. Water not only drove the mill wheels and supplied water for the myriad industrial processes but, prior to the railways, the canals were the main means of transport for goods and people. Most of the lowland rivers have been altered and channelled, but in the Pennines, a number of upland streams were harnessed and their catchments transformed in the service of manufacturing. Reservoirs, mill ponds, mill streams, dams, weirs, channels, settlement ponds, leats and culverts were installed from the late 18th century on, and the remains of these can be found today.

A good example is at Hebden Bridge in west Yorkshire where the river Calder and its tributary, Hebden Water, facilitated the development of a busy textile industry.

These days, Hebden Water and the adjacent Crimsworth Dean Beck flow down a wooded valley from heather-clad moors to join the river Calder in this picturesque town, but in the 19th century, nine textile mills were operating among hills that had been stripped of vegetation. Highest up the Hebden valley was the Gibson Mill which is still intact along with its large mill pond and it is now a popular visitor attraction owned by the National Trust. The industry has gone and the forest has taken over, but many of the structures, channels and ponds remain and have become refuges for nature.

The forest is fairly typical for a millstone grit area: mostly oak, interspersed with sycamore, birch, lime and coniferous trees. The forest floor cover is bracken and many other ferns including great wood rush, along with some bramble, grasses and enchanter's nightshade. At first sight, this is fairly typical acid clough woodland, but there is a lot more going on in and around the many ponds, waterways and industrial remains beneath the trees.

There are brick walls and structures that are festooned in ferns and mosses, on top of which young alder and downy birch trees attempt to take root. There are many marshy areas where **Narrow-leaved Reedmace** *(Typha angustifolia)*, marsh marigold *(Caltha palustris)*, hemlock water-dropwort *(Oenanthe crocata)*, blue water-speedwell *(Veronica anagallis-aquatica)* and other wetland plants compete for light and space. The terrain is steep and rugged, accessed on footpaths which leave the ponds to mallards, coots, moorhens and the fish and amphibians below the surface. One concern here is that, at the time of writing, the invasive Himalayan balsam *(Impatiens glandulifera)* is taking hold. It is controlled where the National Trust owns that land, but much of it is privately-owned and rather inaccessible, making control much less likely.

There are a number of similar locations on Pennine waterways where nature has enveloped the 'dark satanic mills', although the valleys above Hebden Bridge may be the most extensive. Such areas occur in both gritstone and limestone areas and are worth exploring for the history and for the varied plant communities that exist among the ruins.

Water is still used by industries in the Pennine uplands, particularly in limestone quarries of which there are several in the Peak District. As each quarry reaches the end of its commercial viability, the industry moves on leaving behind bare cliffs, flats, ponds, channels and scars for nature to colonise. Wetlands within the quarries are colonised far quicker than the rocky areas, and researchers have found rich communities developing over time.

Narrow-leaved reedmace

MARSH AND WETLAND PLANTS ON PENNINE WATERWAYS

Although most have been drained for farming, many soft banks, bogs and creeks remain along the rivers which are often rich habitats with a different mix of species from the upland bogs. In the springtime, marsh marigolds *(Caltha palustris)* form mats of brilliant gold backed by lustrous dark green leaves on boggy ground and at the water's edge while pale cuckoo flowers wave from the grassy edges. With the summer, the majestic yellow iris *(Iris pseudocorus)*, great willowherb and meadowsweet are in flower and bulrushes reach for the heights while water forget-me-nots, watercress and lesser spearwort flower below. There are also sedges and reeds providing cover for amphibians and water fowl.

The **Butterbur** *(Petasites hybridus)* is a perennial which unusually starts its annual growth cycle with its flowering from February on. This is comprised of a sturdy spike with dozens of round clusters of tiny pink flowers which are an excellent nectar source. Each spike is of a single sex so those in the image below are the larger male flower heads which were photographed in the Calver Weir Restoration Project on the river Derwent. Once fertilised the female flowers develop into seed pods and the leaves swell to great size, often over 30cm.

Butterbur at Calver Weir on the river Derwent

Marsh marigolds in bloom on the River Dove in the Peak District

Yellow iris plants starting to grow in the spring on a bog beside the river Wye in Monsal Dale

Meadowsweet (Filipendula ulmaria) flowers have a frothy creamy character. It can be found growing in calcareous grasslands and meadows as well as swamps and ditches

The pretty blue flowers of the Water forget-me-not (Myosotis scorpioides) are larger than those of the common species

The plant spreads by underground rhizomes and can colonise large areas, as shown in the photograph (below) of the river Hamps in the far south of the Peak District whose dry bed is completely covered with butterbur plants as the autumn approaches. In this case, it is quite normal for the river to flow only underground for much of the year. Water lies just under the surface of the river bed and flows through underground channels in the limestone bedrock.

PENNINE RIVERS

When does a beck become a river? Often when the name changes, or it meets a larger stream: there is no definition, except we imagine that a river tends to be larger with a more gentle flow. So in this section we are focusing on more mature streams which may have rapids or, as is the case on the Derwent and Dove, weirs which were built to control and calm the river flow.

There are also rivers like the Twiss and Doe, which drain the heights of Ingleborough before their confluence to form the river Greta at Ingleton, tumbling down steep inclines and plunging over waterfalls like Thornton Force and Beezley Falls for much of their length. Such rivers behave like large becks and these are covered in the previous section. This section is about the rivers that flow more slowly, where the gradients are gentler and the river bed is wider and often deeper.

The quality and composition of a riverine habitat is dependent upon water quality and also on the extent and nature of human interventions. Where a river is closely channelled between hard walls, vegetation can't develop as it would on damp-to-boggy areas of the river bank, so biodiversity will be much lower than if it were allowed to find its own course. Controlling a river's course keeps it tidier and considerably reduces the amount of land it takes up, as long as the flow remains within normal limits; however, following an extended downpour, if a river breaks its banks, the flooding can be disastrous.

In the light of experience on rivers across the country, views on flood management are changing so that the Environment Agency now has a programme called *Working With Natural Processes* in which the research is applied to determine the optimum way to manage a river to mitigate flooding. The likelihood of flooding on rivers is increased when water is able to run off the land more quickly upstream; for instance where trees and scrub are absent and grazing sheep keep the ground vegetation low.

River Ribble near Sawley

projects. These projects also benefit wildlife through reduced intervention and human presence and the natural development of patchwork habitats where wildlife communities can thrive.

The quality of water in the Pennine valleys has to be closely controlled if it is to be maintained sufficiently unpolluted to support fish and other life. There are widely dispersed inputs from agriculture in the form of nutrients and pesticides along with those from villages and towns, including sewage treatment works, drains, industrial outputs and urban run-off.

The ecology of each river along the Pennines is different and could easily have its own chapter. Discussion here is restricted to where rivers flow through a more or less rural or wooded landscape. Each of the many Pennine rivers has its own character and almost all offer beautiful scenery and great opportunities for enjoying it. Many are shallow, rocky and full of rapids like the Ribble above Settle, while other are calm and gentle like the Derwent at Baslow and they flow through all the landscape types except high blanket bog. Some, like the Dove in Derbyshire or the Doe and Twiss near Ingleton are spectacular and have popular walking routes giving access to the best scenery while others are remote and less visited but fascinating to explore for their varied biology and geology.

Restricting rivers to clear, straight courses with hard banks causes flood water to speed up and often results in even worse flooding below. A river winding through its natural course slows the flow of flood water and the wider channel, where the ground has not been compacted, results in far more water being absorbed into the ground rather than running off.

Scrub and woodland may be planted or allowed to develop and management practices can be changed to take the emphasis off neatness and to give nature back control, often saving a great deal of money spent on hard engineering

WILDLIFE IN THE PENNINE RIVERS

Most larger rivers flow through improved grasslands with uninterrupted grass often to the water's edge, often with trees such as alder and willow growing along the banks. It is usually grazing or mowing that maintains this situation as there are many more species which would readily root in damp, fertile soil on a river bank. In drier agricultural soil the very common species like nettles, brambles, daisies and dandelions may dominate, but where it is wetter, reeds, rushes, yellow irises, ramsons and marsh marigolds will grow. Unfortunately some invasive introductions like Himalayan balsam (*Impatiens glandulifera*) or Japanese knotweed (*Fallopia japonica*), although not yet particularly common in the Pennine rivers, can completely take over a river bank within just a few years, so they need to be removed whenever they are found.

Where a river's banks are wooded, or in backwaters, mosses and ferns are more likely to be found along the

The weir on the river Wye at Cressbrook

river's edge, along with many of the woodland flowers as well as marshland specialists. A lot depends upon whether the area is trampled or grazed, and whether the banks have been walled in to stabilise them. Many of the Pennine rivers are controlled by weirs, installed to stabilise the river and create deeper stretches for angling. In holding back the water, the weirs can result in losing valuable marshes and wetlands in which wildlife can flourish, but they also enable silt to gather and prevent rivers from finding their natural courses which might have resulted in a more interesting and diverse natural community. Whether or not weirs are a benefit depends upon the priorities of those responsible for the river channel. Where weirs can be insurmountable obstacles to fish, in particular migrating trout and salmon, work is going on to remove them or create salmon ladders and passes.

One of the best ways to measure the quality of water in a river is to monitor the riverflies: that is, the quantity and types of river invertebrates including mayfly, caddisfly and stonefly larvae. This is done on a regular basis on many rivers to establish the state of the river in terms of water quality and biodiversity, by the Environment Agency, by volunteer anglers or by local and neighbourhood conservation groups. These insects may spend years as larvae, feeding in the stream-bed detritus, before emerging into an often brief adult life as flying insects. As larvae, they are often predators of other invertebrates but are essential prey of crayfish and fish, which is why their numbers are often followed closely by anglers.

Riverfly species often pupate at the same time and so emerge in swarms on the same day. In the case of mayflies, enormous numbers of insects with striped bodies and glistening wings can be seen doing a sort of dance in the air during the month of May in the UK. Their lives are brief – a few days at best, during which a great many of them are eaten by fish, birds and dragonflies.

A mayfly at rest

Banded demoiselle female consuming a mayfly

The quantity and make-up of fish species in any river varies enormously, but in the cleaner streams can be found any of brown trout, salmon, grayling, perch, chub, dace, roach, river lamprey, bullhead, stone loach, minnow and stickleback.

Brown Trout *(Salmo trutta)* live in many of the Pennine streams and rivers, the smaller ones managing in quite small becks where their main food is crustaceans and insects. Brown trout occur in most of the significant waterbodies across the Pennine hills where the natural population is supplemented with farmed fish for anglers in some reservoirs. There are two forms of the brown trout: one which remains permanently in freshwater, referred to as the *riverine* ecotype and one that spawns in freshwater streams, migrates out to sea during the middle of its life and returns to the stream to spawn in its birthplace. This is the *lacustrine* ecotype which is commonly known as seatrout. Seatrout are returning to British rivers in greater quantities as water quality has improved in the mature lowland rivers that were turned into industrial sewers, not fit for life, up to the late 20th century.

Improvements in the status of our larger rivers, such as the Ouse, Humber and Trent have also enabled **Atlantic Salmon** *(Salmo salar)* to return to the Pennine rivers including the Derwent in Derbyshire, and the Don,

Brown trout

Photographers waiting for leaping salmon at Stainforth Force

and slower-flowing rivers, especially where there are vegetated margins. They feed off a mixture of aquatic plants and invertebrates, and the moorhen can take small fish.

Mallard ducks (*Anas platyrhynchos*) (overleaf) are by far the most common duck in Britain with around 100,000 breeding pairs. Breeding pairs is a rather inappropriate term for mallards as they have a promiscuous mating system and the male plays no part in incubation or chick rearing. They feed by dabbling upended in shallow water as they feed on plant material and invertebrates.

Aire, Ribble and Ure in Yorkshire. To help them migrate and spawn successfully, fish passes are being constructed where weirs and other obstacles exist and local trusts and anglers are at work to improve matters further for the fish. Watching the salmon leap up the rapids and smaller waterfalls has become one of the spectacles in the Yorkshire Dales, for instance on the Ribble at Stainforth Force.

Many of the more or less common and widespread aquatic birds can be encountered on the Pennine waterways. Coot, moorhen, mallard, teal, tufted duck, great crested grebe, little grebe, water rail, and cormorant all visit the uplands as well as the valleys, where they join swans and herons.

Mallards and Canada geese are ubiquitous in British waterways and seem to be rather tolerant of less than perfect conditions, so are the most likely to be encountered. Coots and moorhens are also frequently found, particular where there is cover provided by reeds and other river plants.

The **Coot** (*Fulica atra*) and the **Moorhen** (*Gallinula chloropus*) are in the same family as the water rail and corncrake but far more common, especially on the lowland waterways of England. They are both found in Pennine lakes, reservoirs

Coot

Pair of moorhens

The magnificent **Great Crested Grebe** (*Podiceps cristatus*) and the diminutive **Little Grebe** (*Tachybaptus ruficollis*) are both found most frequently in the southern half of the Pennines, but do appear at Malham Tarn. Grebes are specialists in diving and are rarely seen on land, except when nesting. Their legs are placed far back so that they are very effective as a driving force when underwater and chasing fish. They can also adjust their buoyancy by altering the angle of their body feathers to eliminate air. Little grebes sometimes use this to submerge so that only the head and neck are visible above the water. Great crested grebes feed mainly on fish whereas little grebes are largely

Clockwise from top right: Mallard ducks, Cormorant, Tufted duck, Great crested grebe, Little grebe

aquatic insect feeders. The little grebe in the image is in its muted winter plumage, which becomes more colourful for mating in the spring.

It is safe to say that **Cormorants** (*Phalacrocorax carbo*) (below) are not loved by fishermen as they are very good at catching fish and are becoming widespread on inland waterways. They will be seen, often in groups, their wings spread to dry them while at rest.

The **Tufted Duck** (*Aythya fuligula*) is a diving duck that breeds on ponds and lakes in the Pennines, feeding on a mixed diet of aquatic invertebrates and plants. A male is pictured showing his black and white plumage, but the female is all brown.

The **Goosander** (*Mergus merganser*) is a large diving duck that can be found on many of the wider, wooded rivers in the northern half of the Pennines.

They belong to a group of ducks known as 'sawbills' because their long bills have saw-like 'teeth' which are very effective at gripping small brown trout and immature salmon (parr) as they dive in search of food. Unfortunately, this makes them very unpopular with anglers, especially when water has recently been restocked with trout. They are fast fliers and good swimmers, so are formidable birds.

Goosanders tend to appear on the Pennine rivers in the spring, when they nest in holes in riverside trees where the female carries out all the duties of incubation and rearing the chicks. In the winter, they fly to lakes and reservoirs in the lowlands.

The **Common Sandpiper** (*Actitis hypleucos*) is a small wader that is a summer visitor to the Pennines. It can be seen picking for insects along the rocky shores of rivers, lakes and reservoirs and has a conspicuous white wing-bar which flashes as they fly off.

Above: Goosander

Below: Common sandpiper

Kingfishers (*Alcedo atthis*) occur across most of England and Wales but peter out in the north and Scotland. Despite their colourful plumage they can be difficult to spot as they spend much of their time sitting quietly in bankside vegetation and the turquoise plumage can look dark as it is only the back that truly shines. Often the high-pitched call betrays their presence before you catch sight of one.

They nest in self-dug burrows in banks of almost any waterway that contains small fish. They hunt from overhanging vegetation and plunge into the water when they spot a fish, but occasionally they hover kestrel-like over water before plunge-diving. Kingfishers are highly territorial to protect their food supply during the breeding season but often leave the Pennines in winter when waterbodies freeze.

RIVERSIDE MAMMALS

The mammals are there too, but usually much more difficult to spot. Water voles and **Eurasian Otters** *(Lutra lutra)* inhabit the undisturbed banks of some stretches of river, particularly in the northern half of the Pennines.

Populations of both species are recovering, having suffered badly during the past 100 years. The otter became nearly extinct in England in the middle of the twentieth century because of poor water quality and the effects of persistent agricultural pesticides whose effects remained in one of their favourite foods, eels, for decades. Otter hunting was ceased voluntarily in Britain in 1978, followed by legislation to ban DDT organochlorine and

organophosphate pesticides (Dieldrin and Aldrin, for example) and measures to drastically reduce domestic and industrial pollution of rivers.

As water quality improved, fish returned to rivers and lakes and, as a top predator, the otter population recovered well. Each decade, the Environment Agency has surveyed the otter population across the United Kingdom, with the sixth survey taking place in 2018, and up until 2010, each survey recorded increases in both range and numbers of otters.

When a top predator is reintroduced to an area, there is always the fear that all of the prey species will be consumed, and anglers feared they would no longer have any fish to catch. However, otters can only exist in numbers

supported by the fish population and, if that goes down as happened in the 20th century, then the otter population will crash. In reality, anglers and otters can normally co-exist on the same river.

Top predators also create some unexpected benefits for the local ecosystem, and in the case of otters, one of these is that American mink populations decrease dramatically when otters are on a waterbody. Mink are voracious predators of small mammals and birds, including water voles, whose population falls whenever mink are in the area. However, otters are good at finding mink nests and take their young. Experience shows that mink disappear when otters arrive on a river.

In conclusion, the more mature Pennine rivers have been treated rather badly, especially during the twentieth century, but the worst of the damage has been reversed so that they again support aquatic life. They can be concrete channels, closely linked to industrial canals, gentle rivers between well-managed banks or open, meandering streams which are rich in wildlife. For the time being, it is salutary to realise that few of the rivers in our Pennine uplands achieve better than 'moderate' status, and we must hope and work for a better state of affairs.

Water vole

Where to find Pennine aquatic habitats

Water is pretty much everywhere in the uplands and the large moorland SSSIs, such as South Pennine Moors, Dark Peak, Moor House and Cross Fell, Upper Teesdale and others contain many blanket bog pools, becks and reservoirs; however the list below is of SSSIs which are centred on the main aquatic habitats covered in this chapter.

SSSI name	Location	County	Hectares	O.S. Grid
Combs Reservoir	High Peak	Derbyshire	32	SK 038795
Dovedale Valley & Biggin Dale	White Peak District	Derbyshire	670	SK 157506
Gouthwaite Reservoir	Yorkshire Dales	N Yorks	148	SE 129693
Hamps & Manifold Valleys	White Peak District	Derbyshire	2167	SK100540
Kilnsey Flush	Yorkshire Dales	N Yorks	3.7	SD 972675
Lathkill Dale	White Peak District	Derbyshire	272	SK 187658
Malham-Arncliffe	Craven	North Yorkshire	4934	SD920676
River Derwent (Yorkshire)	Ryedale-Selby	North Yorkshire		SE 678287
River Derwent at Hathersage	White Peak District	Derbyshire	9	SK 209822
River Ure Grasslands	Yorkshire Dales	N Yorks	40	SE 147870
Semerwater	Ryedale	North Yorkshire	101	SD913865
Stoney Middleton Dale	White Peak District	Derbyshire	69	SK 210760
Strid Wood	Yorkshire Dales	N Yorks	59	SE 070560
The Wye Valley	White Peak District	Derbyshire		SK 154722
Topley Pike & Deepdale	White Peak District	Derbyshire		SO 099717
Upper Lathkill	White Peak District	Derbyshire	26	SK 143677
Upper Wharfedale	Yorkshire Dales	N Yorks		SD 965735

APPENDIX

Human Effects On Waterbodies

On both sides of the Pennines lie the towns at the centre of the Industrial Revolution, which was powered by water which initially kept waterwheels turning and was subsequently needed to produce steam to power the engines. It was also used for endless industrial processes, after which it was dumped back into the river, often untreated, badly contaminated and poisonous. Canals were built throughout the region for transport, requiring major changes to the rivers and surrounding countryside, to the extent that canals often took the main water flow.

Industry sprawled up the river valleys and where the rivers weren't diverted to canals, they were channelled between brick and concrete walls, the trees and meadows which had lined them being replaced by liquid waste outlets. So it was that, in the 1960s, rivers like the Don through Sheffield, the Calder through Halifax and Wakefield and the Roch through the Lancashire mills were open industrial sewers containing virtually no life and often dyed a lurid colour.

Since then, legislation has been introduced in stages to control pollution and return to cleaner waterways, culminating in the creation of the Environment Agency in the 1990s, dedicated to contributing to *a rich, healthy and diverse environment for present and future generations*. The Environment Agency was set up to ensure that the water environment is protected, and strict regulations are applied within the Water Framework Directive. However this is European legislation which, at the time of writing, will have to change as the UK leaves the European Union. Even so, the effectiveness of regulation and control of pollution depends upon the strength of enforcement, which requires political will and substantial public funding, both of which vary.

In addition, the nature of industry and its processes have changed, with little heavy industry and producing far

fewer untreated, harmful substances. Regulation along with local action have brought life back to the rivers, although the job of restoring the waterways is far from complete and pressures on them remain from several sources.

Acid Rain

Acidification of waterways can be natural where water seeps out of a blanket bog to join a stream, or semi-natural when fallen pine needles acidify the ground water in a plantation. However the worst problems happen when it is caused by industrial or transport emissions which acidify the atmospheric water vapour. Much of the rain that landed following the Industrial Revolution had been acidified by factory emissions upon which there were no restrictions to speak of until the 1956 Clean Air Act. Further UK and European legislation since then, along with huge reductions in heavy industries such as coal mining and steel, have greatly reduced the carbon, nitrogen and sulphur dioxide emissions so the situation has improved dramatically. Today, pollution from sources like transport emissions, or industrial emissions from Eastern Europe, continues but to a far lesser extent than fifty or a hundred years ago. The controls on emissions continue to develop, prompted by their deleterious effect on human health and on the environment, especially plant life. In the Pennines acid rain caused the loss of sphagnum moss, denuding the blanket bogs, and killing trees. In limestone areas, it also accelerated the erosion of limestone rock, dissolving the calcium carbonate of which it is comprised.

Agriculture

Modern agriculture has come to depend upon the application of a range of chemicals to large areas of the landscape, including fertilisers and pesticides. Fertilisers such as ammonium nitrate and ammonium phosphate (there are many) are extremely soluble in water so can easily be washed off a field or pasture by rain following application. The contamination of ground water by nutrients is now a problem across much of the UK and, where it occurs, it is a chronic problem that is getting worse and will take a very long time to resolve. In addition, these chemicals degrade soil by destroying the legion of invertebrates, fungi and bacteria that maintain its health and richness, reducing the soil's ability to support healthy crops and further damaging its ability to hold on to water.

More dramatic pollution can occur when sediments from animal dung or silage liquor escape from farmland into the channels that feed our waterways or percolate down into the ground water, fundamentally changing its composition. Often the first sign of this is dead fish floating on the river or washed up on its banks, at which point the damage has been done and all that remains is to trace the source. Because of the high concentration of silage liquor and farm waste, this sort of pollution is very severe and remains a risk in the Pennines as there is livestock on much of the agricultural land.

Where artificial nutrients enter waterbodies, the first organisms to take advantage tend to be bacteria and algae of a type which take oxygen from the water. Blooms of red, or blue-green algae can take all the light and are often poisonous, putting fish and much of the 'healthy' river life in jeopardy. Even in lower concentrations, the increase in nutrients alters the mix of organisms which thrive in the water and therefore compromises the entire ecosystem.

There are other widespread pollutants which wash off into the waterways, particularly from arable farms. These include pesticides, particularly metaldehyde which is used to control slugs and snails but in waterways will kill crustaceans, insects, aquatic snails and many more of the creatures that make for a healthy ecosystem. Metaldehyde and some others are being phased out and are less of a problem in the Pennine rivers than in many other areas as the proportion of arable among the farms is relatively small.

Industrial and Domestic Waste

Legislation and policing by the Environment Agency, along with public education about the importance of clean water, have resulted in businesses being very careful about how they use water and what they send back into the rivers. Industrial pollution events do occur and although they have become relatively rare, as with silage, they can be severe and sudden.

The technology behind sewage treatment has meant that water returned to rivers from the outflows of treatment plants is normally of good enough quality not to pose a threat to the river ecology. That being said, there are thousands of treatment plants throughout the country discharging into our rivers, some of which are very large and industrial, some small with a few settlement beds, and also many pumping stations. Ensuring the quality of the discharge requires that the plant is maintained well, and that there is suitable monitoring in place. This may be in the form of full-time, highly trained staff in the larger plants, but is often automated in small plants and pumping stations, in which case there has to be a robust system in place to detect and react to alarms. In this we are dependent upon private water companies, regulated by OfWat and the Environment Agency, to invest adequately and to maintain their staffing and systems very well. With our increasing population and spreading urbanisation, the demands are growing and the well-being of our waterways is dependent upon good resource planning and implementation by the water companies. People in the community also have a major part to play in not wasting water and being careful what they flush down the toilet as the former has an effect on river levels in some areas, and the latter reduces problems in dealing with sewage through preventing the build-up of insoluble rag.

Mistakes and carelessness by companies and individuals still cause problems whose impacts may be relatively local in their effects: but once polluted, a river takes many years to recover.

ENVIRONMENT AGENCY DECLARATION OF THE STATE OF PENNINE WATERWAYS IN 2018

River Name	State	Notes	Direction of Flow
Dane	Poor		West
Doe	Good		West
Don (to Burnley)	Poor	Forest of Trawden	West
Eden	Good	Upper section	West
Etherow	Poor		West
Goyt	Moderate		West
Greta	Good	Yorkshire Dales	West
Hodder	Good	Forest of Bowden	West
Irwell	Moderate		West
Lune	Good		West
Pendle Water	Good		West
Ribble	Moderate		West
Roch	Moderate		West
Sett	Moderate		West
Skirden Beck	Bad	Lead etc. Joins Ribble	West
Tame	Moderate		West
Twiss	Good		West
Wenning	Good		West
Leeds & Liverpool Canal	Good	Summit	Both
Aire	Moderate	Keighley	East
Arkle Beck	Moderate		East
Calder	Moderate		East
Colne	Moderate		East
Coverdale	Good	Joins Ure	East
Derwent	Moderate	From Wye junction	East
Derwent	Good	Above Wye	East

Don & Little Don	Moderate		East
Dove	Moderate		East
Greta	Good	Upper section	East
Greta	Moderate	Mid to lower	East
Hebden Water	Moderate	Moors to R.Calder	East
Holme	Moderate		East
Loxley	Moderate		East
Manifold	Good	Tributary of Dove	East
Nidd	Moderate		East
Rother	Moderate		East
Sheaf	Moderate		East
Swale	Moderate	Headwaters good	East
Swale	Good	Upper section to Muker	East
Tees	Moderate		East
Ure	Moderate		East
Wharfe	Moderate	Lower, from Barben Beck	East
Wharfe	Good	Upper	East
Worth	Moderate		East
Wye	Moderate	Most scenic in Peak District	East

River Wharfe near Kettlewell

SUMMARY OF THE EA FINDINGS

Water quality in rivers throughout England is in a moderate to poor state in all but a few locations. This is due to current pollution from agriculture, industry and domestic sources, but also from past activity where dissolved substances have penetrated the ground water or where metals and chemicals remain on the surface of the abandoned works.

The Pennine chain is a watershed for its entire length, with becks rising in the heights either flowing to the east, through Yorkshire and on to the North Sea, or to the west, through Lancashire to the Irish Sea. The list of many of the Pennine rivers on the previous page shows the state of each in 2017 while it is within the Pennine Hills area. Rivers are rated as having high, good, moderate, poor or bad status, based on their biological and chemical composition. Ammonium (NH_3) and phosphate (PO_4) ions are measured as indicators of organic sources of pollution, such as sewage, and their concentration is expected to be maintained at a very low level. In addition, dissolved oxygen is measured and the composition of the river invertebrate population (river fly) is investigated as indicators of the biological health of a waterway.

In the upper regions of the Pennines, most rivers are in a moderate to good state, but hardly ever in a pristine, or 'high' state. A few of the upland streams are classed as bad or poor because of mine workings, although work ceased over a hundred years ago, or because of particular local circumstances, but these are exceptional. The table gives the Environment Agency rating for each. It should be noted that the stated aim of the Environment Agency is for all rivers to have a 'Good' or 'High' status and therefore to be in a sustainably healthy condition. Waterways that are in 'Moderate', 'Poor' or 'Bad' status are in need of action.

The data shows that the great majority of waterways throughout the Pennines are in Moderate condition, a few are Good and many are in Poor condition. This applies to watercourses at all altitudes, but quality decreases with lower altitude and distance from source. Sadly, in a number of cases the state of the upland waterways has not improved but gone downhill since 2009. This may be due in large part to money and resources being withdrawn from the Environment Agency and Natural England.

It should be noted that a 'Moderate' status is not the default: it means that the river is compromised, but that it can sustain a viable ecology which will be good in places and less so in others. Problems can escalate when the weather is dry and warm as the flow decreases and nutrients can become more concentrated. At the time of writing, the number of pollution incidents reported is increasing and the money to improve the rivers and streams has been decreasing; it is only to be hoped that the environment starts to count more in the Government's calculations if the situation is to be turned around.

The main causes are those described above, but in the uplands, a significant factor is water from reservoirs which is discoloured by peat, so not directly related to human-generated pollution. This is severest when peat is bare and degrading, and is one reason why restoring peat bogs is urgent and important. At a national level, the more serious problem is the increasing presence of nutrients in waterways whose sources are agriculture along with mistakes or misconnections in the sewer network. Nitrates in particular have penetrated the ground water and as their further application to the land continues, reducing nutrients in rivers is becoming somewhat intractable.

That being said, efforts are being made on streams throughout the Pennines to conserve and improve them, and a number of the rivers, especially in the north of the region, support healthy ecologies and a wide range of species. At a local level, voluntary groups make a huge contribution to conserving the natural environment, although the territories covered are often very small. In this, the rise of voluntary rivers trusts and their involvement in Catchment Partnerships and their engagement with the water companies is a welcome development.

TIM MELLING PHOTO CREDITS

All other photos by the author
Doug Kennedy, except:

ACKNOWLEDGEMENTS

I am indebted to all of the people who contributed to putting *Wildlife in the Pennine Hills* together. The book was inspired by my love of the Pennines which I first explored when studying biology at Sheffield University.

It is also inspired by the photography of Tim Melling, the brilliant Yorkshire naturalist and photographer. Since I started this work, Tim has been extraordinarily generous in sharing his encyclopaedic knowledge and in supplying hundreds of photographs which make up the core of this book and furnish much of the beauty and biological detail that it contains. His knowledge of nature in the Pennines, where he lives, is astonishing, and he was always patient when helping me get the detail of each species correct: I learned that the depth of understanding of someone whose life has been devoted to studying the natural world provides by far the best insight.

The final chapter on waterways is mine alone and proved to be particularly tricky to put together because, as I got into it, the subject grew and grew. I am very grateful to Professor Philip Warren of Sheffield University who provided feedback on the early drafts and helped me to shape the unruly mass of information into a usable and comprehensive form. I am also very grateful to Jim Wright, Head of Studies at the Malham Tarn Field Studies Centre for assisting with advice, equipment and species identification.

Doug Kennedy

BIBLIOGRAPHY

Collins Bird Guide, 2nd Edition, Lars Svensson (Collins, 2009)

Dragonflies & Damselflies of Britain and Ireland, Steve Brooks and Steve Cham (British Wildlife Publishing, 2014)

Green Guide to Butterflies of Britain and Europe, R Goodden and R Goeden (New Holland, 1992)

In Pursuit of Butterflies, Matthew Oates (Bloomsbury, 2015)

Butterflies of Britain and Ireland, The, Jeremy Thomas and Richard Lewington (British Wildlife Publications, 2014)

Concise British Flora in Colour, The, W. Keble Martin (Ebury Press, 1965)

Wild Flowers, Sarah Raven (Bloomsbury Publishing plc, 2011)

Wilding, Isabella Tree, (Picador, 2018)

Yorkshire Dales, John Lee (William Collins, 2015)

Curlew

INDEX